PE SPEED RE
ET
LOAD
US
AH
VE H
TIO
PPED P
No ENT
PLEASE QUE
BE ST
LI
AS MIND TA
POSITION CL
CLOSED DUE TO REFURBISHMENT NO AC
BATTERIES NOT INCLUDE
KEEP OFF THE GRA
GS ALLOWED NO CHILDREN ALLOWED L
WHEEL CLAMPING IN OPERAT
OPERATION NO BALL GAMES CAR P
LINE-ALL OUR OPERATORS ARE BUS
PLEASE HOLD OR TRY AGAIN LA

THE
Angry
Island

THE
Angry
Island

Hunting the English

A.A. GILL

Weidenfeld & Nicolson
LONDON

First published in Great Britain in 2005
by Weidenfeld & Nicolson, a division of
the Orion Publishing Group Ltd
Orion House
5 Upper Saint Martin's Lane
London
WC2H 9EA

1 3 5 7 9 10 8 6 4 2

A CIP catalogue record for this book is available
from the British Library

ISBN 97 80297 843184
ISBN 0 297 84318 4

Typeset by Deltatype Ltd, Birkenhead, Merseyside

Printed in Great Britain by
Clays Ltd, St Ives plc

The Orion Publishing Group's policy is to use papers that
are natural, renewable and recyclable products and made
from wood grown in sustainable forests. The logging and
manufacturing processes are expected to conform to the
environmental regulations of the country of origin.

www.orionbooks.co.uk

This book is for my mother, Yvonne Gilan, without whose good breeding and astute timing I might well have been born one of them.

CONTENTS

Acknowledgements

I need to thank Mark Getty, Joan Washington, Jeremy Clarkson, Sandy Nairn, Alan Samson, Lucinda McNeile, Michelle Klepper, Grainne Fox, John Sutcliffe, Emily Sutcliffe, Paul Raben, Alex Bulford and Nicola for their help, advice and experience, all of which were invariably sage and germane and just as invariably ignored. None of them should be tarred with responsibility for the opinions here – they are all mine alone and you're welcome to them.

Foreword

This is a collection of prejudice. Opinions based on a lifetime's experience. Identifying what it is that makes a nation a people and not just a random collective of individuals who happen to share the same geography is a risky business, but we all know that nations are recognizable and different from each other. It's almost too obvious to dispute that Canadians are not like Brazilians and the Irish are not synonymous with the Jews. A national character, when self-defined, is the stuffing of patriotism and pride. It is also the source of umbrage when the observation is made by foreigners.

The English are the most enigmatically indecipherable people when seen from outside. Even from the inside, what is definable isn't always understandable. Their homespun enigma is itself part of the carefully engineered English mythology. When I was first considering writing this book, an American said: 'Oh God, please, write an owner's manual for the English. We look at them and they're so familiar, but so alien and weird. I have no idea how you make or repair an Englishman.'

This isn't quite an owner's manual, but it is a series of observations drawn from having lived amongst the English but never having felt one of them. This is not a book of facts. Facts are inert things. Facts are what pedantic, dull people have instead of opinions. Opinions are always interesting. What people deduce and make out of their own lives is what attracts and informs. Never mistake a fact for the truth. The English, of course, are inordinately fond of facts – they hoard them and throw them through the windows of home truths. But facts are only the scaffolding, the trellis up which bright opinions are grown. So don't look for proofs here, there's precious little forensic evidence. This is just what I know to be true.

1

The Angry Island

'Is England like this?' I looked out of the dusty window at the red earth and the swaying blue gums. The acacious scrub along a drainage ditch was an equivocal ribbon of slum that occasionally bulged into a sprawl of shanty suburb. That unmistakable global vernacular. The architecture of invisible people. In the distance vines neatly engraved the curves of rolling hills; all basked under the deep azure sky.

We were driving out of Cape Town. The taxi-driver, who had kept up a desolate monologue for an hour, a well-thumbed and threadbare litany of homespun irritation, suddenly asked: 'Is England like this?' Like this? No, not really. Not remotely, actually. The question was laughable. Few places are as precisely not England as the southern tip of Africa. He was an Afrikaner, a Boer. An old man who bitterly clung to the bottom rung of his own tribe's hierarchy and was now being squeezed and threatened by the pressure of these squatter camps and the turn of history's screw. This was probably the epitome of some kind of England for him – that other pale tribe who had colonised this land. The Cape was the heart of English Africa. Ten minutes earlier, we had passed a memorial to that archetypal Englishman Cecil Rhodes, a statue of a heroic man on a horse which, weirdly, is a cast of one called 'Physical Energy' by George Frederick Watts that I walk past on wet autumn Sundays in Kensington Gardens.

'Well, what is England like, then?' he asked, and the tone was just the other side of polite tourist's enquiry. I continued to stare out of the window. I didn't want to get into the unstated current of this conversation. What is England like? I dipped into the bran tub of trite and came up with hedges. Hedges and sheep. He snorted. We drove on in silence.

It's a question that's been tugging my sleeve ever since. What is England like? I'm a member of that post-war generation who first grabbed the benefit of cheap and easy international travel. Our parents went to the seaside, the Lakes and the Dales; we went to the Balearics, the Cyclades and Kathmandu. And then swiftly leap-frogged the globe.

We didn't do England, unless it was to visit relatives or go to school. I can recognize the England in the Cape or in Simla, Hong Kong and the Costa Brava. Those little deposits of Blighty that are by turns charming, absurd and embarrassing. But the original, the real England, I only see occasionally through the dreary window – from the motorway or train, or on the television. It's familiar from books and magazines and conversation, but secondhand. A strangely alien place. It's a shock to realize that I'm more familiar with East Africa than I am with East Anglia. One of the reasons I've travelled as much as I have is because of Kipling's rhetorical question: 'What should they know of England who only England, know?', but a Boer taxi-driver made me think that I don't actually know England at all. That begs yet another rhetorical question, how can you truly know where you're going if you don't really know where you've come from?

Now, some months later, here I am at the edge of England. This is where it starts. And if the cloud hadn't crashed, I'd be able to see some of it. Today the weather has got so fed up and lazy it can't even be bothered to rain with panache. It's just lying here on its back being wet. I suspect if you ask most Englishmen where England started, they'd say Dover. The White Cliffs.

Named by the Tourist Board 'Shakespeare's Cliffs'. What could be more English than Shakespeare and chalk?

This is the chalk that the Continent is cheese to. This is the bastion, the great white wall that separates the 'them' from the 'us'. This is what has made England first and last. It's an island. Everything that's English stems from this apartness. Except – point of order here – England isn't an island, it's half an island. And I'm not standing at its southern tip, but at its northern end. For me and the other half of this island, England starts up here, on Hadrian's Wall. No one ever says Scotland's an island, though it is just as much one as England is.

Hadrian's Wall is only a great big disappointment if you come to it without expectations. If you visited it with a completely open mind, it would be distinctly underwhelming. Possibly one of the most underwhelming experiences of an unexceptionally uneventful life. It's a peasant's outward-bound park of signposts.

The English are addicted to public labels. I've never been anywhere that has such a pressing need to subtitle, footnote and instruct the particular. Hadrian's Wall's labels draw your attention to things that aren't there, but might once have been. So we all slither along, looking at invisible gatehouses, barracks and communal lavatories. It would be funny if it weren't so damned sheep-shit miserable. But of course, us natives don't come here without expectations. We have heads full of them. We can see it all, the Eagle of the Ninth, the legionaries huddled in their cloaks. We can smell the peaty fires, hear the centurion bark orders and the cohorts march past – dexter sinister, dexter sinister. We look North with a weary weather eye, over the great defensive ditch for signs of the fearsome-painted Scot. In our collective imagination we understand that this isn't just where England begins topographically; it's where, for that long rumpty-tumpty epic, England really kicks off. Hadrian's Wall is the first page. The start of history. Before the Romans there were some mythical 'them', and after the Romans, it's the beginning of 'us'. Never mind that this was actually Italy's garden wall built by Germans and garrisoned for the most part by poor bloody Belgians, it's England. A cliff at one end, a wall at the other.

Having their creation myth begin with the Romans has been very important to the English. It gives them the straight road in the soul and a birthright of order and rigour. A stoic square jaw, stiff lips, noble brows, steely eyes, deaf ears, sure hands, beating breasts and well-planted feet. England's moment as the most distant, nebulous, unconsidered and unimportant afterthought of a decaying empire allowed the English to pretend that Latin was their spiritual first language and put up statues to their great and good dressed in togas. It also gave them permission to have a classical revival once a century. And, most important, this little servile touch of the *Pax Romana* gave them the model for their own defining achievement, the blessed Empire. Hadrian's Wall may have been built to keep the Celts out, but now it keeps the classicisms in.

Just beside the Education Centre and Resources Gift Shop, huddled in the lee of the wall, is a little refreshment kiosk, a couple of puddle-white plastic garden chairs and a hatch that dispenses tea, Coca-Cola and KitKats. Maureen, a lank-haired plumply-pretty schoolgirl is bored to rocking distraction by this grisly Saturday job. She's sitting her exams this summer and her ambition is to travel. The ubiquitous wish of the young, to be somewhere else. I rather like this little hole in the wall, it's the most authentically ancient English thing here. There must have been stalls like this 1800 years ago and Maureenish girls dreaming of getting away. There's a sign that recommends sandwiches made to authentic Roman recipes – well, who could resist? I ask for a chicken one. Maureen wrinkles her nose and hands over a polythene wrapped pocket of pitta bread that oozes a vivid chemically-yellow lumpy slime. Anywhere else, it would be Coronation Chicken with turmeric. At the first bite the seams of the pitta burst and I'm holding a palmful of viscous slurry that plops onto the ancient Roman paving stones and my mouth's full of a simpering goo. Vile. Yet somehow evocative. The origin of the bread is Greek, the mayonnaise French, the spices are Asian, the chicken Indian. But all together the concept, the construction and the flavour could only be old England. This is where England really begins, with this speechlessly polyglot, misbegotten cod-historical sandwich.

I'd better come clean. You may have suspected I don't like the English. One at a time, I don't mind them. I've loved some of them. A lot of my friends were born here between the cliff and the wall. It's their collective persona I can't warm to. The lumpen and louty, coarse, unsubtle, beady-eyed, beefy-bummed herd of England. And although I live here amongst them and have done for virtually all my life, although I sound like an effete middle-class paragon of them, I've never been one. Never thought of myself as one. After more than fifty years of rubbing up against the English, I still resist assimilation. I don't stick out, but neither do I fit in. My heart doesn't syncopate to 'Land of Hope and Glory'. I don't want three lions on my chest or the cross of St George on my windscreen. I've never been moved to bellow the theme from *The Great Escape* whilst watching a game. The truth is – and perhaps this is a little unworthy, a bit shameful – I find England and the English embarrassing. Fundamentally toe-curlingly embarrassing. And even though I look like one, sound like one, can imitate the social/mating behaviour of one, I'm not one. I always bridle with irritation when taken for an Englishman, and fill in those disembarkation cards by pedantically writing 'Scots' in the appropriate box.

I was born and part bred in Edinburgh. When I look out over Hadrian's Wall I'm looking homeward. I only lived there for a scant year of my life, of which I remember not a thing. But still it's the place that raises in me all that sentimental porridgey emotion that England can't reach. Scotland is the home of my heart. I'd rather have a bouquet of thistles than roses. Scotland is a country and a people whose defining characteristic is built on the collective understanding of what they're not. And what they're not is English. Difference is all comparative. To be different you have to be different from something, or someone. The Scots are different and, it goes without saying, better than the English. But having said that I don't feel English, neither do I recognize the caricature that the Scots make of the English to underline their Scottishness. That snobbish, stuck-up, two-faced, emotionally retarded, dim, foot-in-mouth prat and his good lady. The truth is, I don't know what it is that makes the English so dreadfully English. So impervious to fondness, sympathy or attraction. I've been searching for a national characteristic, or a basket of characteristics. There is a familiar problem with the English. They lack a single image, an instantly recognizable mannequin to hang their character on. It used to be the bowler-hatted, umbrella-wagging Civil Servant, but no one under the age of forty has ever seen a bowler hat worn seriously. There are no universal cultural icons. There's just tons of culture.

The English are great collectors and curators of culture, perhaps more than any other people. They love nothing so much as a glass case full of numbered bits and pieces. But all this stuff deflects rather than reflects who the English really are. And they're no help themselves. Ask them what an Englishman is like and they'll probably go, 'Well, um, you know, sort of nature's gentleman.' OK, what's the definition of a gentleman, then? 'Um, an Englishman. Not being French.' The lack of a national logo has periodically niggled the English, particularly at points in their history when cohesion seemed important. The Victorians spent a lot of energy and pulpit time trying to define Englishness. They saw that not having memorable brand recognition was a problem. Everyone else seemed to have a pithy label, a subtitle. The French of course were vain, the Germans bellicose, the Italians excitable, the Spanish proud. Americans were optimistic, Orientals were wily, Arabs were shifty – and then there were a lot of off-the-peg monikers that could be awarded like birthday honours to the lesser nations of empire, when the need or event demanded. Plucky, valiant, devoted, loyal, stoic. But what could we say of the English. 'Nice manners?'

So the Victorians set about constructing an idealized Englishman. He was clever though not intellectual, worldly but shy, moral but not judgmental and, above all, fair. If the English could award themselves one attribute it would be fairness – as in sporting, though not necessarily sporty. Australians could be sporty. Sporting fairness is an English obsession. You may recognize the composite character that embodies all these dreary virtues. He is the hero of dozens and dozens of Edwardian schoolboy novels written by ageing Victorian men. That prig, who taciturnly plodded and punched his way through hectic adventures, overcoming foreigners and duplicity. But despite the best efforts of Englishmen, he remains a fiction. You won't recognize him in the street, the factory or the pub. Fairness, though, is a recurring English concern, whether it's embodied in referees, High Court judges or gun boats. So perhaps it's a good place to start. But actually I think it's the wrong way round. What the English are eternally concerned with isn't fairness, it's unfairness. There's a constant mutter of grievance at the deviousness, mendacity and untrustworthy nature of the rest of the world that has moulded the bottom half of this island.

Not being able to put your finger on a national character doesn't mean it doesn't exist, and the thing that seems impermeably English is, in fact, anger. Collectively and individually, the English are angry about something. The pursed lip and the muttered expletives, the furious glance and the beetled brow are England's national costume. A Pearly Queen's outfit of thousands and thousands of lovingly-stitched and maintained irritations. A simmering, unfocused lurking anger is the collective cross England bears with ill grace. I can see it in English faces, in the dumb semaphore of their bodies. It's how they stand and fold their arms and wait in queues. It's why they can't dance or relax. Anger has made the English an ugly race. But then this anger is also the source of England's most admirable achievement – their heroic self-control. It's the daily struggle of not giving in to your natural inclination to run amok with a cricket bat, to spit and bite in a crowded tea-room, that I admire most in the English. It's not what they are, but their ability to suppress what they are, that's great about the English. The world is full of aggrieved people whose fury engulfs their land and lives. Places where feuds and retaliation have become the sole motives for existing. But the English aren't like that. They live and have always lived in a comparatively harmonious and liberal country. There is more give and take and compromise in England than anywhere else you can think of, but I know as certainly as I know anything about this place that this is *despite* the nature of England, not because of it.

People with therapists will tell you that repressed anger is a dangerous thing that in the end will consume the repressor. That it's a spiritual, emotional cancer. That it must be evacuated like trapped wind, transformed and metamorphosed. But the English are an uncomfortably living testament to the benefit, if not the pleasure, of repression. They have come up with dozens of collective and individual strategies to deflect and contain their natural fury. Not least, in inventing a bewildering number of games. It's not in the games that the English excel, it's in making the rules that govern them, and the committees that oversee those rules. It's in controlling the consequences of unbridled competitiveness. Only the English could in all seriousness say: 'It's not whether you win or lose that counts, it's merely taking part.' If the result is secondary, why bother taking part in the first place? But of course, for the English, just getting off the pitch without their opponent's ear in their pocket is a personal victory over their natural national inclination. And it's their anger that has made them arguably, over the long run, the most consistently successful of all the old European nations, certainly the most inventive and adventurous and energetic. Controlled anger is the great impetus to achievement. You have to do something with it. Anger simply won't let you be comfortable in your own skin.

The English aren't people who strive for greatness, they're driven to it by a flaming irritation. It was anger that built the Industrial Age, which forged expeditions of discovery. It was the need for self-control that found an outlet in cataloguing, litigating and ordering the natural world. It was the blind fury with imprecise and stubborn inanimate objects that created generations of engineers and inventors. The anger at sin and unfairness which forged their particular earth-bound pedantic spirituality and their puce-faced, finger-jabbing, spittle-flecked politics. The English have, by the skin of their teeth and the stiffness of their lip, managed to turn what might have been a deforming fault into their defining virtue, but it still doesn't make them loveable.

I dumped my sandwich in the bin labelled 'Litter' and left the Wall. This isn't exactly the border anymore, which has moved up and down since the Romans left – mostly up. This bit of the country, Northumberland, doesn't feel very English. It's an anonymous hard, darkly dour land. But then neither does it feel Scots. For most of the time since the legions left it has been neither or both. A bad land of reiving and raiding. A place of private power and shifting loyalty. The border country on both sides owed allegiance to itself rather than to the thrones of London or Edinburgh. It's all been made rather swashbucklingly romantic now by the Tourist Board, and the village post offices sell border ballads and folklore pamphlets. Reiver's mustard and Rustler's toffee. But not many tourists are drawn here. It's an arcane and gritty little local history that's never caught the imagination of the south; only the most devout walkers navigate the sodden moors and the endless criss-cross of stone dykes. The north-east isn't on the way to anywhere anymore. Whatever wealth and manmade beauty it had is burnt or buried. And the sense of place is anything but romantic. For a thousand years, this must have been the most unpleasant and frightening corner of the British Isles. The stark and still terrifying pele towers are its defining architecture. In Hexham, where the bishop once had his own army, the squat bunker of the abbey exhibits the chipped and bashed remnants of a mailed and muscular Christianity. You know that this must have been a hard place in which to be a devout turn-the-other cheek Christian, and a despairing place if you were not one. In the toll booth that was once a magistrate's jail, there's a tatty museum to reiving, with tipsy mannequins wearing amateur dramatic costumes and mothy nylon wigs. A local amenity that doesn't so much make the past live as show how half-hearted and poor the present is. History gave this place a kicking, and it isn't about to pay compensation by way of tourism.

I watch a football match on TV in a pub. Bony, thin men with lager-pregnant stomachs bellow sing-song expletives at the screen. Their hands are permanent fists, nicotine knuckles punching the air or throttling bottles. Even on a Saturday lunchtime the atmosphere is thickly aggressive. Flint-faced lasses with lank home-dyed hair, sloppy bosoms and bruised thighs slouch round-shouldered over lime tops. Their eyes dart smugly, knowing that even the plainest of them could start a bone-spattering fight with the merest wink. There's a story in the local paper. In the outskirts of a village just up the road, a father and a son lived in a bungalow surrounded by eviscerated cars, marred and twisted industrial detritus. They were builders, dodgers, make-do-and-menders. 'Quiet,' said their neighbours. 'Kept themselves to themselves.' Up here in these tight-lipped communities, that must have been arctic quiet. Extreme apartness. The son built a full-sized working guillotine in his bedroom, its blade weighted with paving stones. He rigged up an electric trigger to the clock radio, blew up a lilo and lay on it beneath the guillotine. At precisely three in the afternoon the blade fell. His father found him that evening. How can two people share a bungalow and one build a guillotine without the other knowing? But it's the electric trigger that really grips. Imagine the long grey evenings tinkering with wires and catches. The quiet pride gilding the despair, the testing and the standing back and admiring, the job well done. Then blowing up the bed, settling down, watching the ceiling and waiting. Was the radio already on? Did he listen to the local traffic conditions, a request for 'Candle in the Wind', a phone chat with a local farmer about sheep prices? Did the station jingle play as they ran up to the three o'clock news? Did he have time to think that next day, as Northumberland trudged on, he'd be the headline? Did he take a quiet satisfaction in knowing that he was joining the long march of local history and dying by the blade? Welcome to Northumberland, where folk keep themselves to themselves. The insistent whisper of this place creeps up on me, like a chill in the night. I understand what the keening atmosphere is. It's not romantic solitude, it's not self-reliance, it's just a terrible, terrible, sad, silent loneliness.

Flodden is just the English side of the border outside the little town of Wooler. I can't imagine many people come here to this field of autumn roots. Why should they? There's nothing to see, just a stone cross, erected during the Victorian memorializing boom. I doubt that one Englishman in a hundred will know what happened here. Again, why should they? In the march of their rich tapestry it's barely a dropped stitch. But from my side of the border, this, as they say about football pitches, is hallowed ground. Here was the greatest defeat of the Scottish Army. That pibroch that pipers always play at funerals, 'The Flowers of the Forest', that's about what happened here. This was where the flowers of the forest were cut down in 1513. It was the equalizer, the home-game decider for Bannockburn. Henry VIII took his vaingloriously Renaissance Prince fantasies over to France for a bit of a poseur's slapping match on the Field of the Cloth of Gold, and James IV of Scotland, mindful of his responsibilities under the Auld Alliance with France (though breaking his Treaty of Perpetual Peace with England), marched across the border as an act of Catholic solidarity. It wasn't much of an invasion. He meandered about the marches as a gesture. It doesn't even appear to have had a destination. But an English army was dispatched and they met here. The Scots weren't just beaten, they were thrashed, routed and massacred. James died and much of the Scots aristocracy with him.

There are any number of Glasgow pub theories as to why the Scots came off so badly, having started off with the high ground. All they needed to do was wait. But, piecemeal, they charged down the hill and were cut to confusion. Perhaps the long and unfamiliar French pikes Louis had sent as a house present – and that James felt honour-bound to make his army use – were to blame? Perhaps the Scots, with their customary lack of discipline or ability to see anything more than red, threw away their unassailable advantage. Or maybe half the armies on both sides were borderers and stitched up the result between them. But in fact you know, looking across these neat fields of English cover crop at the nicely maintained pheasant woods, that the Scots lost because losing was what they were used to. And the English won because it was their destiny to win. With a particularly Celtic touch for piling on the pathos, the news of a great Scots victory had already been galloped to Edinburgh. The church bells were still clamouring when the horrible, predictable truth limped back across the border.

Flodden was the crucially mortal blow for Scotland. You could say it was here that the best chance of Scotland surviving as an independent nation state dribbled into the mud. From hereon, it's a straight and stony path to the exhausted and shabby anti-climax of the Act of Union. James may not adorn as many biscuit tins or ballads as Bonny Prince Charlie, and Flodden may not be as memorable as Culloden, but the high romance of the Young Pretender was just a postscript to a story that to all intents and purposes ended here for no good reason. If you look at the history of Scottish kings from the time of the Norman Conquest, barely one died in his bed, or came to power in an orderly manner. James IV was the best hope the nation had had in three centuries. He was clever and civilized. He was popular and the closest thing the north got to a Renaissance Prince. The country, for once, was peaceful and united. Edinburgh was beginning to become a wealthy cultivated capital and, crucially, he was married to Henry's sister. Their union would lead to the uniting of the island.

After Flodden, Scotland was once again flung into confusion. The new king was an orphaned infant, the big neighbour once again a meddling enemy. Why did James risk so much for so little, for the pathetically one-sided Auld Alliance, which had always done so much to harm Scotland and meant so little to France? The reason seems inescapable. The Scots simply reverted to type. Danced to the drum of an ancient tune that always ended in stalemate. It is in their nature to conspire in their own confounding. They hadn't even been beaten by the English king himself, but in his absence by his missus.

The battlefield is pretty and benign in the chilly sunlight. Down the road is a squat church with a maudlin air. This is where the dead and dying were brought. Around about are the jumbled ossuary pits in which they buried Scotland's forlorn hope.

I don't know why I'm so drawn to battlefields. Like a morbid picnic, you have to bring with you whatever it is you expect to find there. But, living in England so long, I've caught the English disease of history: the desire and the ability to overlay the current with a film of the past that is supposed to explain and rationalize, but actually shadows and distorts. I've gone on about Flodden because it's indicative of two approaches to the past. For the Scots, as for so many small countries with powerful neighbours, history is something that's done to you. For the English, history is something you do to others. That's a vital keystone of Englishness. No other country cultivates and harvests the past to serve the present as single-mindedly and comprehensively as the English do, and I envy them that.

Absolutely nothing in the whole world gives an Englishman a more quiet, wriggly, warm, smug pleasure than to have an American say, 'What I love about your country is that it's got so much history, so much more than we have.' Other nations may have more power, wealth, sunshine, sex and better food, but you just can't buy a past. You can't retrospectively manufacture breeding. But then of course you can, and the English have. It's a perfectly obvious truth that every square mile of the earth has as much history as any other. We all have the same number of ancestors, and all nations have the same amount of time to pick over and edit into a national plot. But the English, of all countries in the world, have made their story the premier epic. They've cornered the market in top-of-the-range history. History is the map that shows you how you got here. It can also be a useful guide to how you might continue. But it's a map that keeps moving, and a set of instructions that are being constantly rewritten. How the English stole history is one of the great unsolved crimes.

The central belief of Englishness is that they were made by their history. History is the anvil and the hammer was England, and the English. That nations are made by their history is what emerged from the fire. Actually, the truth is quite the reverse. England has conspired and invented a history that suits and comforts it. History is a moveable wake. It dates as fast as science fiction. It's a great English conceit that their past is written in granite, whilst pretty much everyone else's is written in sand. Having lived this long with the English reverence for the gay pageant of time, I'm always astonished by how little the Europeans make of history and with what ease they will, and indeed can, discard the trappings and links to the past to make way for the convenience and comfort of the present. They seem so cavalier with it, so spendthrift. For the English, discarding the past is like spending capital. Eating seed corn. In England, changing the shape of a telephone box evokes a fury that might be justified by grave-robbing.

It was whilst I was writing a story on Germany that I realized what I think is a fundamental difference between English history and everyone else's. England hasn't actually had that much history, and what it has had has been comparatively bland and picturesque. The past is still a pleasant country for the English to visit and ruminate over and make up national fairy stories about. There is nothing in England's story that can compare with the vicious and painful millennia across the channel. They have never experienced a thirty years war or an Inquisition. There were no Cathars or Huguenots. No struggles for independence, no ebb and flow of invasion. The two World Wars were experienced on a completely different level from the rest of Europe. Since the Norman Conquest, with the exception of the Civil War, English history is mostly something that the English did abroad.

What I noticed in Germany was that, because their national story was so painful and guilty, the Germans have divorced their political past from their cultural past. They find their national pride through music, philosophy, science and literature, which exists in a chronology that is separate from their disastrous political history. It also means that there was a Germany in art and thought long before it appeared on the map. This would simply be impossible in England. Culture and history here are indistinguishable, indissoluble. In the minds of the English they amount to the same thing, so that you will often hear them say with great authority and utter conviction that the trouble with European states is that they don't have much history as countries. They're only in the infant school, whereas the English have the mellow sagacious clear sight of being of a great age, an impeccable vintage. The only dispensation in this over-weening patronage is to countries that have had to fight them.

What is so extraordinary about this utterly self-serving and bogus view of history isn't that the English believe it is gospel, but that almost everyone else seems to as well. When national characteristics and talents were being handed out and the French got style, and the Germans got order and the Italians got being Italian, the English got history. Partially, I suspect, because, being a worn-out and dead thing, no one else wanted it. But it was a canny choice, like buying up the world's back catalogue. Owning history has given the English many things: a sense of purpose, a near biblical identity, and been there, done that smugness. But above all, it's given them justification. History justifies their prejudices and makes their slow anger righteous.

Like almost everything else, the English invented the rules of history. Naturally, they first claimed a classical precedent from the Greek Herodotus and the gossipy imperial Roman propagandists. The seminal text of English history isn't about England at all, it's about Rome – Gibbon's *Decline and Fall of the Roman Empire*. Its cut-glass elegance is a master class in Englishness. You couldn't imagine a book that was less Italian. It reasserted the claim of Classical Rome for Blighty and was a guidebook for the nascent British Empire. The English lifted history from being memory, hearsay and supposition, and organized it into an idealized hybrid of science and art. Constituted on empirical foundations, but decorated with Corinthian flourishes.

There is no doubt that the English manage history more beautifully and inspiringly than anyone else. They've made it their beautiful game. And you don't have to be a crabbed old academic to have a go. Essayists, stylists, journalists, poets, mystics and novelists have all taken up history and created a canon of splendid grandeur. The facts are handmaidens to the style and the effect, and towering over it all is Shakespeare. Revered, avoided, quoted, unread. He gave the English their national legend. He was England's Moses and led them to a land of retrospective milk and honey.

Despite all that, your average Englishman knows precious little history, and what he does know is probably handed down the ancient Homeric way, as anecdotes via the troubadour television. It's a disjointed hotch-potch mythology of heroes and events. But that doesn't matter. History is what surrounds an Englishman from the day he is born. It's everywhere. Like the pictures on medieval church walls which promoted the Glory of God for the illiterate, so England is a cartoon strip illustrating the propaganda of the past. Anything with the merest, faintest antiquity is preserved and listed and labelled. In England all our yesterdays are ever today.

2

Face

I have no idea why I was chosen. A Monday morning letter, *sotto voce*, conspiratorial, a word to the wise – would I agree to be included in the collection of the National Portrait Gallery? Just like that. No explanation. No why or wherefore. An opaque reference to some board who had agreed that I should be elected. And there you are. There I was, blindsided by the Establishment.

I spend a soft socialist bespokely egalitarian lifetime girding myself against flattery and public displays of vanity. I have filed away in the back of my head the letter I would courteously write to turn down a Birthday Honour. I have developed a fox's ear for sycophancy and pray nightly for the power to 'just say no' to the bouquets and decorations of social elevation. It's their thing, not mine. It's an English thing.

I've seen and reported on it so often. Watched with an undisguised sneer the flushed faces framed by a rented top hat, with the proud wives in silly mother-of-the-bride outfits outside Buckingham Palace, holding up the little enamelled brooches and grinning that awful grin of the grown-up caught doing something embarrassing and childish: getting a milk monitor badge, being made prefect, awarded sporting colours. The little back-hander from the Honours system, a badge that says: 'I worked all my life to do something good or exceptional or brave and all they gave me was this bit of tin on a nylon ribbon, and this photographer is charging me £100 for the photograph of me looking like some Queen-fixed dupe, completely chuffed and utterly gormless.' Bought off by three minutes of patronage.

I know how to sidestep that sort of thing: the initials after the name, the honorariums, the letterhead inscriptions, the little embellishments on wallets and shirts and linen. The dangling luggage labels of premier service and extra social legroom. I'm wary of all that – and then this comes out of the green baize door and whispers, 'Would you like to be part of the National Portrait Gallery?' The deep, thick, rich tapestry of great English achievement.

No one has ever declined. You just can't say no. There's no overt benefit here, money doesn't change hands, you can't charge more for your services afterwards, you don't have to wear a silly hat, but this is how the Establishment gets you. Of course the Gallery denies that it's Establishment. It smiles its inclusive smile and points to its walls. Here are rogues, poltroons, chisellers, revolutionaries, the amoral, immoral, corrupt and corrupting. You'll feel quite at home here. But I knew when I said, 'Oh yes please' that I'd crossed some line, that an invisible velvet rope had been unclipped to let me pass. I had gone from the *us* to the *them*.

They wanted a photograph. I had it taken by Terry O'Neill with an enormous Heath Robinson Polaroid camera. I liked the implication of instant and disposable. Black-and-white achievement – it seemed right for a journalist.

Having been charmed into being hung with the grand and the cool in a fit of excessive anti-hubris, I never went to see it. I kept meaning to and then it was gone. Sunk into the deep reserves of the collection. I doubt it will ever resurface. But my daughter saw it on a school trip to the museum. She told me that they'd turned the corner and she'd exclaimed: 'There's my daddy!' 'Oh, is it someone who looks like your dad?' says the teacher. 'No, that is my daddy.' A little choking, Railway Children moment. And that's how vanity and patronage and the Establishment get you. We will all look absurd, swallow principles, step on heads and fingers, and doff caps to impress our children. It's not even the marble of posterity, just the fleeting admiration of a thirteen-year-old. So, what did you think? 'Well,' she said, 'You looked kind of mad.' Angry? 'No, loony.'

The Establishment is a peculiarly English concept. An oligarchy, a club, a freemasonry of like-minded and self-serving people. Usually men who run the institutions of the nation with a quiet rectitude on behalf of themselves and the status quo and a quiet life. The word Establishment comes from the Church. The established Church of the nation. Establishmentarianism is the promotion of a state Church, and that word beloved of sixth-form debaters and satirists, 'antidisestablishmentarianism', means those who oppose the disestablishment of the state Church.

The secular Establishment was a much bigger deal for my father's generation than it is for mine or will be for my children. For the men who came back from Hitler's war, the Establishment was a fifth column whose purpose was to thwart the changes of a new order and a new world. The Establishment tried to derail the Health Service. It was the nabobs in the Foreign Office who attempted to hold up the dissolution of Empire. For my dad the Establishment was the class system. A secret service. It represented everything they fought to change. The marvellously English thing about it was that no one knew who was actually a member. The Establishment was a secret society without a roll call. There were people, of course, who were *de facto* members: judges, bishops, generals, Whitehall civil servants, consultants, presidents of royal societies. And then there were the lackeys of the Establishment: NCOs, magistrates, doormen.

To accuse someone of having become a member of the Establishment was a dire insult. Peter Cook called his club the Establishment as a joke. The Establishment never met in secret conclave, never had public rallies; its members never referred to each other as Establishment figures. It was like a great castle, and only those on the outside could see the extent of its walls and fortifications. On the inside, it just looked like a collection of agreeably inoffensive nineteenth-century rooms. The Establishment was gentlemen's clubs and Mayfair restaurants, Members' enclosures on race tracks and cricket grounds. It went to the country at weekends, shot and fished and rode and played golf, and, with winks and raised brows, pursed lips and tapped noses, it gently chivvied and guided the nation like a flock of slovenly sheep.

There was no corner of the country too insignificant to attract the interference of the Establishment. People would put their blighted careers down to their refusal to kowtow to it; planning permission and the price of beer and the pick of the England team could all be ascribed to and blamed on the Establishment. It was the most perfectly English invention. It only existed because everybody agreed it did. There is a road beside Buckingham Palace called Constitution Hill. We don't have a constitution, and it isn't a hill. The Establishment was an empty name that was given supernatural powers. The English particularly like institutions that have grown without rules or written agreements. They like the world to be unframed – a society formed from precedent and common practice. Heritage and good manners are far more compelling than a contract or a rule book for the English.

The Zulus have a sprite, a goblin called *tokolosh*. It comes out at night and climbs up your bed leg. A *tokolosh* is really, properly frightening, not just a bedtime story. And the reason it's so specifically terrifying is because everyone makes their own. A *tokolosh* is a bespoke demon constructed out of your deepest fears and insecurities. It knows you. It is the homunculus of your darkest thoughts. The Establishment was the *tokolosh* of the English, a construct of all their insecurity and snobbery, a spittoon for their anger and the slights of life. They were all joined together and made a regiment of faceless, pin-striped demons.

The Establishment's great role was part of the coping mechanism for English fury. The nebulous will-o'-the-wisp nature of it meant that it could stand as a huge punch-bag and sponge for self-righteous anger. If it had been any more visible or corporeal, it might have ended up strung from lampposts or bottled outside pubs; but you couldn't sue the Establishment, or ask it outside man-to-man. It soaked up the resentment and never tired. It subtly altered its methods and its membership as society changed its demands. It came up with new frustrations, and then, without any of us noticing – some time in the late eighties – the Establishment stole off into the night.

It was as if we'd all grown out of it, stopped believing in it. The trappings of the Establishment are still there: the titles and the clubs, the royal societies, the conventions, the dining-room, the Members Only bars, but they no longer broker power or influence. The Establishment may have disappeared in one incarnation, but the collective need for something like it is still here, and in many ways the role has been taken on by the monstrous battalion of celebrity.

From the outside, celebrity looks like a closed shop, a mutually beneficial oligarchy whose rules are unspoken, whose members are elected by some secret ballot. All celebrities seem to know each other and live in a world separated from the rest of us by an invisible rope of privilege and preference. Celebrities get things done. They can make and change things. People listen to them. The simple power of their fame can alleviate poverty, bring peace, water deserts. They fill in where the Establishment left off. Where the Establishment was anonymous, celebrity, by its nature, is not. And the anger that was once directed generically is now specific.

Look at the walls of the National Portrait Gallery and you can trace the drift from the great and the good to the famous. I'm sitting here at my desk surrounded by English faces, staring up at me in a not entirely friendly manner, accusing eyes looking over ermined and tweedy shoulders. They're all dead. It's a random eliding, a memorial montage window into the English.

I went to the Gallery and like all educationally-insecure, easy-listening compilation intellectuals, I can't resist the postcards. In fact, for many the National Portrait Gallery is merely the farm that supplies the postcard shop: here is Vita Sackville-West snuggling up to Joe Orton. They look weirdly similar, they have the same sort of face, the head slightly cocked, the mouth pursed, half camp, half irritation. They're both gay, of course. And the eyes, like barrels of a shot gun – not nice, not kind, not remotely interested. If you lived in England for a month you'd know them both from the instant their eyes met yours and glazed over. Sackville-West, for all her Sapphic mystery, all the belles lettres, the puppy love of ugly menopausal women and that sodding garden – the middle-class Englishwoman's Gethsemane – you can tell she's one of those micro-tempered, corridor-minded, multi-storey snobs. A dry stone tower built of pre-conceptions, ancient gossip and comforting fibs. She had an irrational, opinionated snobbery about everything: flowers, poetry, cushions, shoes, horses, cooked fish, writing paper, adjectives and who your daddy was. And you look at Orton and you see the same thing; the prejudice and the self-righting beliefs are consigned slightly differently, but Vita could be Joe in drag. Both see themselves as small, precious gems set in a slagheap of dross.

Sackville-West is caught in a winningly ghastly outfit: a very bad hat for her face, an oversized gold collar, a shrugged tweed scarf, a hint of pearls, very nasty coral earrings and slapped cheeks. It's very Gloucestershire Oxfam, and all done with such obvious care, such studied bad taste. Orton is contriving much the same effect by wearing nothing at all except the chair that Christine Keeler was photographed in.

The picture was taken by the same photographer, Lewis Morley, two years later. Here's Christine in that iconic pose. Actually, what's really iconic is the chair by Arne. It's been rather bashed about by the time Orton gets his leg over, presumably by people going, 'Oh is this the Christine Keeler chair?'

Keeler is such a regular stereotype. Anglo, Magdalene – a common plot device in the island story. Look at her flinched face, the big hair, the hint of a pout and those same black, gun-barrel eyes. Orton, West, Keeler. All very English characters in the annual panto production of merry England.

Behind Christine there is quite a different face. Looking over his shoulder from under the brim of a slouched fedora with a weary curiosity that is older than the fine features of his face, with its salubrious mouth, is Isaac Rosenberg. This is one of the most beautifully revealing and questioning self-portraits in the gallery, and painting wasn't even what he did best. He was one of that handful of great, great war poets:

> A queer sardonic rat,
> As I pull the parapet's poppy
> To stick behind my ear.
> Droll rat, they would shoot you if they knew
> Your cosmopolitan sympathies.

That's from *Break of Day in the Trenches*, a mortal genius poem written from the front line in Flanders in 1916. Rosenberg was killed in 1918, the self-portrait was painted in 1915, the year he joined up. He was a private, small and sickly. The son of an East End tailor. He was Jewish. He calls himself English in the poem, but wasn't an Englishman that Sackville-West would have recognized, not a man she'd have offered a tour of the White Garden to.

There's a bat-squeak warning, a prophetic note in Break of Day: *'they would shoot you if they knew Your cosmopolitan sympathies.'* What he's referring to is the rat crossing no-man's-land to fraternize with the Germans. But *cosmopolitan* is also one of those country-house code words for Jewish – said with a little smile and a knowing sideways glance – not unlike the glance that Rosenberg questions himself with in the portrait of a tailor's boy who knows his cloth, in this grey suit with the blue spotted tie and a dashing hat, about to wear the khaki that will be his last suit.

I must have bought the postcard of this picture a dozen times. I've had it somewhere near where I work since I was a teenager. We went to the same art school, Rosenberg and I, the Slade. Rosenberg died on 1 April, the day, by coincidence, that I stopped precipitously drinking. I have now lived nearly twice as long as he, but he'll live far longer than me. When they asked me to be part of the Gallery collection, it was Rosenberg that I first thought of.

Postcards of the great, creative and interestingly obscure are like telling rosaries for humanists. For all of us who have unread book lists in our heads that nag with guilt and the sins of omission, buying the photograph of James Joyce or Sterne or Carlyle counts as a sort of indulgence. I stood and watched for half an hour whilst women dithered over which images of the great and the brilliant might say the most about them as invitations to the book club or get well cards. Well, Sam Taylor-Wood is obviously modern and stylish and not too pretentious and Beatrix Potter's safe; Jane Austen is intellectually unim-peachable – but what a plain, sulky little face. She looks like the nanny, and you know that she would be the girl who you could never quite have to proper dinner parties because she'd be too clever by half and not pretty enough by half. Byron's a bit obvious, Robert Graves is better – we simply loved *I, Claudius*. Oh, and Clement Attlee to show we're really disappointed with

New Labour, but that our hearts are sentimentally in the right place even though physically they're with BUPA.

When Gutenberg invented movable type and printing for the West, he found the thing that made his pumpernickel and butter wasn't writing, or the relatively inexpensive dissemination of ideas – the masses not having had access to schools or books before were mostly unable to read. What they wanted were pictures. Little wood-block prints of saints, kings, heroes and naked women pretending to be mythical. These wood cuts were art for the culturally aspirational. They could be carried round in your pocket, a symbol of your intellectual and theological good intent. They were postcards. And postcards promise to fulfil exactly the same function today.

These mass-produced imitations of art and achievement betray the insecurity of the nouveau cultured and auto-tasteful. They are the catflap to our snobberies. Of course, we don't have the excuse of being illiterate. Despite myself I cannot resist a museum postcard rack. For fifteen minutes I can be a miniature Medici, a Berenson, a fake Saatchi. The National Portrait Gallery's postcards are full of double intellectual cholesterol, because they are not just about selling dolls' house art, but the association of great deeds as well. So here I buy Pitt and Huxley, Chaplin, Princess Di and Ralph Fiennes. They add a little glitz and gravitas to my tapping, offer an invisible psychic blurb to the paperback edition.

Back in the Gallery shop an old man with a runny nose walks slowly up and down the alphabetically collected dream team. After an age of indecision, he tentatively reaches out and takes a handful of Augustus John's drawing of Lawrence of Arabia – nice choice. Seven postcards of wisdom.

The first meeting of the Trustees of the National Portrait Gallery was held in 1857. It set down the rules of admission. Members must be dead for ten years. No portrait should be admitted unless three-fourths of the Trustees approved of it.

They were a club offering membership to the worthy and the uplifting, the glorious dead, and this club was to be the pantheon of England. This is England's catacomb, England's CV. The other island nations of Britain and its dependencies and empire are allowed a frame or two, but only as far as they reflect England's glory.

The Trustees further stipulated that they would look at the celebrity of a person rather than the merit of the artist, and they would estimate the celebrity without bias – political or religious. Nor would they consider faults or errors, even if admitted on all sides, as sufficient grounds for excluding any portrait that might be valuable in illuminating the civil, ecclesiastical or literary history of the country.

This was a very English rule. A gallery where the paintings matter less than the subject – how very neatly that dovetails with most Englishmen's art appreciation; asked what sort of painting they like, nine out of ten will say horses or nudes or sunsets. The subject is the point, and so the subject of the National Portrait Gallery was to be the genius of England. The great though not necessarily the good. This was a clever caveat. You can imagine the committee casting a weathered eye over Byron, Emma Hamilton and most monarchs, the rows with nonconformist parsons. If decadence and decency were to be taken into consideration, you could have fitted the collection into a council flat. Greatness and goodness rarely go together amongst the English or anyone else. Palmerston said that the National Portrait Gallery's purpose should be to encourage citizens to review England's Olympians so that they could go away and emulate them. He believed that simply seeing the face of greatness couldn't help but inspire more greatness. The National Portrait Gallery was the first of its type in the world, and there still are only three others – the Smithsonian in America, one in Australia and a Scottish one in Edinburgh. It was a characteristically Victorian act of high braggadocio.

As well as enthusing under-achieving locals it was also meant to awe foreigners. How many countries could fill so many rooms with so much brilliance? Whatever corner of the world you came from, it asked, does your blood run to this much genius in this many disciplines? And, it is, before and above any criticism, an impressive collection that spans every conceivable department of endeavour. Other nations might be stronger in particular positions, but none could muster such a starry team right across the park, although it helped that the English also wrote the history of greatness so that, while the world would be familiar with Nelson and Drake, they probably don't know which admiral won Lepanto.

The new National Portrait Gallery was given a small budget, and the landed aristocracy and mercantile class were encouraged to scour back corridors and spare bedrooms for pictures to donate. The first was, appropriately, Shakespeare – the Chandos portrait. The only likeness that can claim to be contemporary and the only one that doesn't make the Bard look like a Brummie accountant. It is number one in the catalogue.

All portraits are numbered in order of acquisition. The earliest painting is a not very good picture of Richard III. Richard begs a question: 'Where do the English start?' If the Gallery is an exhibition of great Englishness, then why begin with this prince-smothering divisive usurper? Where the English actually kick off has always been a bit of a problem for the English. When do the ingredients of Celt, Dane, Angle Saxon and Norman stew together to become recognizably homogenized English? Alfred was the first monarch to call himself King of the English, but his nation was less than half the country. Perhaps the beginning should be marked by the Diet of Whitby.

England was an ecclesiastical unit before it was a political one. 1066 is a convenient date, but it begins 200 years of colonial occupation. Chaucer can more usefully be used as a starting line. He is the intellectual choice. A mongrel people became English when they began to speak a language that is recognizably English. But for the Victorians and the National Portrait Gallery, it's Bosworth; the death of Richard III and the entry of the Tudors. The end of the Middle Ages and the beginning of that journey that leads directly, and with a smooth upward trajectory of achievement and victory, to the apex of the Queen Empress.

The English are not so much a cocktail of mongrel blood or a creation of geography or a clerical convenience of religion, they are a state of self-belief, an idea of bombastic arrogance that begins in the last half of the fifteenth century. It's a confidence that grows into a sense of divine entitlement. By the middle of the nineteenth century, being English becomes a synonym of success to the point where the Victorians are seriously trying to prove the divine superiority of the English by tracing them back to the lost tribe of Israel and proclaiming a family tree that proved that Victoria was a distant cousin of Christ or vice versa. It must be said that almost all primitive people think themselves divinely wrought, singled out and special. Often their names translate simply as 'the people' or, like the San bushmen of the Kalahari, the first people. But this is a symptom of primitiveness; attempting to prove divine biology in the nineteenth century is the anthropological equivalent of a society regressing to sleeping with the lights on. It may seem embarrassingly absurd, not to say eugenically bonkers, but it was a popular enough parlour myth in England to get most middle-class English boys circumcised. So for the High Victorians, England proper emerges from the gloom of the Middle Ages just in time to join in the Renaissance.

The picture next to the apprehensive maligned Richard is the man who did for him, Henry Tudor. Painted by an unknown Flemish artist, probably so that he could beg a daughter off the Holy Roman Emperor Maximilian I. Henry is really a chancer, a gambler; he's riding his luck. Margaret of Savoy didn't add her lustre to his loins or reign, and in four years he was dead. Henry the Welshman has a foxy cunning look, the little black eyes squint back at you, and you can tell he could be alternately unctuous and poisonous in a heartbeat. He's not a king, he's not remotely regal – far too shrewd and aware to have been born to a throne. He lacks the thick arrogance of primogeniture. Henry was, though, one of the best rulers England ever had and one of the few who left more money than he found. He also left the country Henry VIII, the Renaissance prince, the great monster of self-confidence who staked out the future of New England plc.

Royal portraits are a large part of the National Portrait Gallery's collection. The litany of monarchs, that sing-song mnemonic forms the punctuation and chapter headings of England's story. Here the rooms divide into royal houses and, while some of the pictures are important, the monarchs seem to glide by with a lofty irrelevance. Henry Tudor doesn't look like a king because he looks interested. The rest of them are increasingly remedial simpletons who've been dressed up. They lift their corpulent fleshy faces skyward, the dim eyes betray no internal life; caught in historic poses, they point at invisible symbols and metaphors that will be added later, along with the landscape they lord it over.

Kings pose like inert dolls, surrounded by allegory. Heads of state are a painterly problem. They're not people, they're empty vessels that the blessed oil of monarchy is held in. If they were either ordinary or extraordinary then anyone or someone special could be one. Either way, it would question the hereditary principle.

Monarchs have to look serenely confident and disinterested with an airy wisdom. Entitlement shines out of Charles I's stubborn face. Stubbornness is the only virtue available to the really thick man. His father was James I and VI – a dour, coarse Scot. Charles had Rubens paint the massive allegory of the Divine Right of Kings on the ceiling of the Mansion House, so that to visit him you'd have to walk under this magnificent, confused picture of deified monarchy with added goddesses, tits and arse, looking like a collision between the Old Testament, *Playboy* and a mixed grill; and then right at the end you'd spy James, this dark, surly, complaining little Scotsman with all the charm of a wet Wednesday in Dundee.

They led his incompetent, stubborn, shivering son back out underneath his ceiling to knock his dumb head off. James's grandson, Charles II is a sybarite sick of sin. The black Stuart eyes are hooded with ennui and secrets. He's nearing the painful end of his life, he's about to die of a bad goose egg and a lot of excruciatingly incompetent doctors. He clearly no longer believes in the divinity of anything.

Between him and his father is Cromwell, Robert Walker's wartless picture of him in armour with a rather nancy cummerbund being tied on by a servant. This was painted about the time Charles was executed, and Cromwell has had himself rendered in the manner and style of a monarch-in-waiting. He's doing that lazy, pointing thing with a marshal's baton. Behind him in the sky, storm clouds move away to reveal the blue dawn a-coming. If God's not exactly on Cromwell's side, then at least Cromwell is on the side of God. It's a picture that reminds you of the end of *Animal Farm*, pigs become men.

The problem with rendering monarchs for posterity reached its acme of absurdity in Holyrood House in Edinburgh during the reign of Charles II. An artist called James Dewitt, a Dutchman, caught adrift in Auld Reekie, desperate for commissions amongst the parsimonious Scots who disapproved of displays of vanity and papish idolatry, must have been overjoyed when he was summoned to see the keeper of the king's cash with a view to brightening up Holyrood. What he was presented with and agreed to was possibly the worst contract ever signed by an artist.

On 26 February 1684 he agreed to paint the portraits of 110 kings in large royal postures. He had to do them in two years, supplying his own canvas and paint. The fact that the subjects were all dead and there was no record of what they looked like might have been a boon – a deal of them probably never existed at all. But poor Dewitt had to wade through them, one and a bit a week for two quid each. They are his masterwork. In fact, apart from some fancy paint finishers in Holyrood, they are his only known work. The collection still hangs, dark and wild-eyed, down a long corridor. They are unimpeachably the worst collection of portraits in any place, anywhere. Their sheer numbers do nothing to mitigate their singular coarseness. They look like nothing so much as a school of mental hospital fantasists, or hammy character actors. Many people notice how uncannily similar monarchs separated by hundreds of years appear to be – there is nothing uncanny about it, it's the sheer, tearing hurry.

Why, you might ask, would anyone want such a thing as the mythical kings of Scotland painted by a barely competent starving Dutchman? As if they were a test on some TV quiz show, their purpose was to give Charles the weight of ancestors to confirm his right to be king. The Divine Right had let his dad down. This display of blood and precedence would give him the authority to rule. The hereditary principle is, after all, only a matter of self-confidence and sperm.

After Charles II, the royal jig in England is all but up. Kings and queens come on looking madder and weirder and fatter. Their chins recede, their eyes bulge and their uniforms become more panto than marshal. They're small men lost amongst the faces of their smarter subjects, ponderous and pompous, swept along by a country in a hurry.

As we arrive at the First World War, the royal family is trying to hide in the masses. They have the hunted look of princes who've swapped clothes with their gamekeepers and secretaries, hoping to slip away unnoticed ahead of the mob. George VI eating breakfast with his family looks like an illustration for *Country Life* advertising a posh B&B.

No one is quite sure what a royal portrait is for any more. In three floors of the National Portrait Gallery you travel from Elizabeth I and her frankly disturbed desire to be seen as a Protestant Madonna, through the stripping away of Divine Right to the increasingly thin glory of the Germans until it disappears altogether in William IV, and Queen Victoria re-emerges like a little Gothic revival matron, the mascot on the bonnet of the motor of state that's being built, piloted and driven by the frenzied, messianic enthusiasm of the second half of the nineteenth century.

The last serious royal portrait in the collection is the Annigoni of Elizabeth II. At the beginning of her reign in the early fifties, there was an attempt to record her as the reincarnation of her namesake, the first Elizabeth, as a portent that this could be the beginning of a second Elizabethan age. A new start when the English would clear away the broken pieces of the worn-out infrastructure of their wrecked Empire and bombed, exhausted country, and with blunt tools and rationing begin afresh to produce the nation of Drake and Raleigh once again. Another unstoppable swell of greatness would rise up and drench the world with England's glory.

It's telling to compare the famous Marcus Gheeraerts picture of Elizabeth I with the Annigoni of the second Elizabeth. Number one stands on the map of England, a colossus, a pale Queen Kong, a body of impossible dimensions. She looks like a transformer, a machine that will metamorphose into a human-oid robot. Her little face points out at you without emotion, she has become a living allegory and behind her the leaden sky crashes with thunder and lightning.

There is no doubt here that Elizabeth I is a good thing, and 400 years later Elizabeth II also stands in a gloomy landscape. It could be dawn, but equally it might well be dusk. The land is blasted and empty, her body is covered in a pyramid of a cape against the cold, against the wind of change. She looks to the side, to the right, to the past. Or maybe, perhaps, just out of the window in some soulless official reception room, out at the incomprehensible hoi polloi. Elizabeth II stands in England's ashes. She looks like a refugee, lost and stoical, where Elizabeth I is manga-regal, superhuman. Number II is frail and ordinary. The cloak is not the magic mantle of entitlement, it's just wool; the insignia of the garter is a brand logo on a product. It's a striking image that's grown better with age.

When I was an art student we despised it with a haughty loathing, Annigoni was the terrible warning of what happened to an artist with a retro-technical talent and snobby patronage. But it's a clever picture; it seems to say one thing but there is an ambiguity in it. He understands that his painting of a monarch is not a record of a person, but a time capsule of an age, and he must have been aware of the First Elizabeth upstairs. They fit together like bookends, the start and the finish of the grand age of the English. From the first Elizabeth's grandfather to the Second Elizabeth's father is the great rise and rise of England and the English. In that 400 years is the high age of the twelve most energetic, inventive generations that have grown out of any place in the world, ever.

The point of the National Portrait Gallery was never royalty, it was those twelve furious and innovative generations who made England's glory. Palmerston said that he wanted a gallery where ordinary people could come and be inspired by looking at the faces of achievement. The Gallery was to be the grand national equivalent of those framed photos in fast-food restaurants showing the employee of the month. These are England plc's employees of the age, and it's an idea that poses some fundamental questions and challenges a lot of national assumptions. First it assumes that success, genius and achievement all look like something. That you can see what it is, and recognize it in someone else. And also that it's a look that's *earned*, one you're not born with, that your face grows into achievement, brilliance, genius or bravery; that these things will be recorded in your skin, in the glint of your eye, the curl of a lip and the flair of a nostril; that they will be the tattoos and scars of your tribe.

The Victorians were keen on this sort of thing, they liked phrenology, the science of identifying head bumps, and they compulsively measured and recorded the physiognomies of prisoners to decipher criminal propensity. The idea that greatness could be achieved and was not simply a matter of blood or divine intervention was quite a subversive one; it undermined the right of aristocracy and and monarchy by implying that greatness might be a matter of individual achievement.

The Gallery hoped to show that England was the soil where achievement grew stronger and taller than in any other nation. The Portrait Gallery premise is based on a new way of measuring the birthright of a people: you aren't born to an immutable position in society – the rich man in his castle, the poor man at his gate – you have the free will to make the most of your life, and you will have the added benefit of being able to call upon the collective greatness of your predecessors. So whilst genius is singular, it can also be acclaimed as a plural achievement – Nelson is the victor of Trafalgar, but all Englishmen share his credit simply by being English.

This quasi-scientific, partially democratic, wholly sentimental way of squaring the individual with the collective is something the English are particularly adept at exploiting. Greatness's by-product was Englishness. Everyone had a piece of it, and if need be they could reach out and grasp it. Every Englishman was a Chaucer or a Woolf, or might become Palmerstons and Nightingales, because if *they* could, then we all could.

Every nation believes versions of this, but for the English it isn't simply wishful thinking or an academic patriotism, it's an article of collective trust. And the Gallery does make a very convincing argument for the eugenic richness of the gene pool.

It is also – perhaps intentionally, perhaps simply by necessity – a gravid celebration of the middle classes.

The middle class is a necessary by-product of the original binary class system. When there were just two classes, there were those who did all the work and those who owned all the land. Originally they couldn't even speak to each other. The land-owners were Norman, the peasants Anglo-Saxon or Gaelic. But between these two great social wheels there was a small oily class, a lubricant of clerics and scribes, quacks, bankers and priests, and the very few professions that weren't tied to a manor or the land. These people grew in the cracks between serf and lord, they exploited and multiplied their small advantages and husbanded their power, and by the time Henry II achieved the throne, the middle class was a nascent force in the land, and the Tudors the start of the middle-class muscle that in three reigns would have drained the resources of the court and its patronage and be demanding more opportunities, more equity and more power.

This 400 years of English greatness from Bosworth to the Blitz is the story of the expansion and rise of the middle class. And that is no coincidence. The Gallery is not only an Old Boys memorial to the achievement of England, it is also the celebration of the values of the middle class, the benefits of education, the inquisitiveness of discovery, the potential of invention, the self-improvement of the arts, the pleasure of aesthetics and good taste, the necessity of law and the fairness of commerce and public wealth.

All these can only grow with the middle class. Apart from the martial heroes, royalty and colonial service, virtually every face along these walls is a testament to middle-class values. This is the bourgeois cathedral of achievement. England is indeed a nation of shopkeepers. Their success can also be ascribed to some fortuitous inventions that got England into industry ahead of everyone else. But this begs the question, why did an industrial revolution happen here? England was the first nation to develop a sizeable independent middle class along with coal and iron and railways. This was partly a result of the hybrid, mild form of Protestantism that the English settled on, and the fact that the business-owning class had real political power. The rest of haute Europe, with the notable exception of the Dutch and Swiss, had hierarchies that despised and resented middle-class achievement. The French for example, expelled and massacred the Huguenots, not because they didn't believe in transubstantiation but because they were better business people than their Catholic counterparts.

The English understood the value of an entrepreneurial class, and managed to avoid a revolution at that delicate moment of industrialization where the middle class might have been blamed for working-class woe. England's success is the story of its bourgeoisie, and it's appropriate that the Gallery starts with the first properly middle-class king in Europe, Henry VII.

The assumption of the Gallery is not just that achievement and goodness has an identifiable look in the way that the aristocracy always believed nobility had a look, but that the English themselves have a face in common. As you walk down the corridors there is a certain gaze, a hazy collation of features that seems to grow familiar. There is a propensity to chubbiness, and there are at least twice as many chins in each gallery as there are noses, and only half as many cheekbones. There is a coarseness of feature, a fleshiness of chops and thin mouths. But it's the eyes that you notice more than anything, the eyes that follow you round the room. If there is anyone who still secretly thinks that the swivelling eye of a portrait is a miracle of painting but has been afraid to ask why, let me tell you – any figure painted looking straight ahead will appear to follow you round the room. It's not skill.

There is a particularly good picture for testing this in the National Portrait Gallery. *The Somerset House Conference* is a formal portrait of ten Tudor men sitting at a red carpeted table, each staring out at you. It commemorates the signing of a peace treaty between Spain and England. I first saw it when I was about eight. You approach the picture from the left and a guard in the room told me to look at it carefully, then walk past without a sideways glance, and once at the other side of the room I was to look again. Not only had the eyes of all ten men apparently turned to face me, but the whole table had been picked up and turned round. It was one of the great cultural moments of my early life, this mammoth trick.

Even at that age I knew which side of the table were the Dons and which the English. On the left the Spanish had a beaky, haughty, European mien; on the right the English aren't that much different in terms of their facial hair and uncomfortable ruffs, which seem to make all the Stuarts look like pigs' heads on plates, but there is something about the eyes, a hint of yobbery behind the finery, a confidence born not of Castilian aristocracy and fine breeding but from a sense of thuggish entitlement.

On the walls, more than any similarity of muscle and bone, there is a collective expression that the English wear, and apparently have done so for the last 400 years. It is enquiring, confident and guarded, the way a bull by a gate might regard you. The English stare out from the walls of stately homes and pub signs, and high on the panelling of town halls and university refectories; from vicarages and town houses and bedsits the faces of the English look down on you with a quiet aggression, a hooded confidence.

The English like to be surrounded by themselves. They are clubbable people. Portrait-painting is the quintessential English plastic art. Painting in itself has always been suspect in England as something foreigners do, and if you want it to be good, you get an Italian or a French one. English culture is so unevenly matched against the grandeur and vitality of its language that it's difficult for other mediums to compete – except for portraiture. The English have more portraits than any other European nation. It suits their particular form of timid philistinism. The English mistrust art; they don't like its emotional incontinence, its operatic voluptuousness, and they feel uncomfortable not knowing what it is they're supposed to be looking at. They like a thing to mean the same thing to everyone, like a chair or a steam engine does.

The visual arts are a foreign language that has to be learnt like French, and the English like to have a collective response. That most English school of painting, the Pre-Raphaelites and late Victorian studio artists, annotated their pictures with quotes from poetry and the classics, so that people knew what they were getting. Portraiture suits the English because there is a single, obvious, universal criterion by which it can be judged, and everyone can have an opinion. You don't have to be able to speak like a French perfume salesman, for the truth of a portrait stares you in the face and follows you round the room. It either looks like someone or it doesn't. It's either straight with you, or it dissembles. It has precious little to do with art, but a lot to do with skill and craft, and the English have always valued craft above art, skill above imagination. Portraiture is art for the art suspicious.

Continental portraiture is usually about grandeur, self-proclamation. The portrait is the summation of life, it's a memorial, it's having your trumpet blown for eternity. If you don't want to be looked at, then why have yourself painted? The painting should make you look like a god if you wish to share the same glazed eternity as the pantheon of classical heroes and deities. You should look your best and accentuate the positive. Even the Low-Country portraits of extreme black-and-white Protestants have a severe, mortified swagger to them. But the English seem to take a particular pleasure in being surprised by portraiture. They arrive at their pictures as if by accident or at least under duress; they will be painted in magnificent surroundings but dressed for riding or gardening; they will sit among the talisman symbols of fame and achievement, but in their bedroom slippers with their hair all on end.

Only the English combine this show of power, prestige and bombast with a look of surprised incompetence. To a European this is both bizarrely admirable and incomprehensibly ridiculous, like being able to rub your tummy and pat your head at the same time. It is also coruscatingly infuriating. Such a painted pose, spoilsport humility, is designed to piss on everyone else's harmless and well-earned vanity. Why shouldn't you have yourself rendered grander than you actually are? Why after a lifetime's hard work shouldn't you flaunt a bit? Why does this Englishman have to come along dressed in his foul old tweed coat and sneer at us like we were some flock of ridiculous ornamental chickens?

The English do love their ostentatious shows of dowdiness. The apogee of stateliness is for a duke to be mistaken for his gardener. English generals regularly affected the dress of their soldiers, like Montgomery, the vainest of men, with his tank beret and sheepskin jacket; or the staff officers at Waterloo and the Crimea who turned up in hunting kit with umbrellas. Being good at things while appearing completely hopeless is a joke which never ceases to amuse the English, they just love ragged billionaires, tongue-tied orators, engineers who are baffled by can-openers, plutocrats who are bullied by their dailies and admirals who are sea-sick. What they can't bear are men who boast, who show bravado, who try too hard. It's often pointed out that England is the only country in the world where 'intellectual' is a term of derision. But so is 'professional' and 'expert'.

How they could have arrived at this patently false and ultimately tiresome ever-so-humble gavotte is a bit of a mystery,

because only the English affect and polish the cult of sham-
blingly inappropriate amateurishness with such relentlessly
steely application. It is perhaps part of the defence mechanism to
deflect anger and confrontation. Boasting leads to bellicosity and
jealousy to murder – better to shrug and say it was nothing, or
better still apologize for having managed the thing at all. Self-
deprecation diminishes the achievements of others by comparison and this can be immensely gratifying to the English. It's a
sort of local variation of *schadenfreude*, but there is also a
uniquely English joy in wallowing in understatement. This is a
taste that no other culture I'm aware of has ever achieved or
courted. The English hug themselves with unctuous joy at the
sight of a Nobel laureate who says that really it was all nothing,
just a little formula he came up with in a traffic jam to amuse the
children.

This stoical humility is also the last remnant of a classical
education; it was the mark of Spartans and your Romans to
suffer in silence, that all honour belongs to the state. And the
English have an inflated opinion of the nation. There is an
obvious contradiction here – how can a collection of stumbling,
blushing, gauche amateurs come together to become this
implacable, unbeatable, steely nation boiling over with bellicosity and confidence? Well, the English have thought of that.
Rather than every individual being the embodiment of the
nation's glory, like the Roman or the Spartan, the multiplication
of Englishmen changes them into something else. When they all
join up – like Clark Kent becoming Superman – they morph into
a superhero nation. All those Bertie Woosters become John Bull.

Throughout English fiction there is the model of a shy retiring
man of the shires who is pushed too far and becomes an
Englishman. A chemical change, a collision of galactic forces,
causes a change at molecular level and then by God, Johnnie
foreigner, you'd better stick your head between your legs and
kiss your arsehole goodbye, because this righteous English fury is

biblical. That is the clever thing about the composite English-man. He needs a catalyst, some added ingredient to come alive. What he needs is foreigners.

Walking around the National Portrait Gallery, you are on one level entranced by the roll-call of brilliance, invention and genius, and at the same time aware of the formidable collective power and arrogance that it embodies. One of the accepted rules of portrait-painting used to be that expressions are coarse. Laughing, scowling, crying or frowning, whilst true to the moment, are masks of real character. The honest inner life of a face is only to be found in repose, but of course sitters are not naturally relaxed, they're sitting for a portrait, which is not the same thing. There is a common intensity, a scrutiny. It's a sub-conscious transference from the artist to the subject; the painter is looking with a concentrated gaze so the subject looks back. There is, as you walk through the rooms, the growing, uneasy sense that it is not you viewing the pictures, but the pictures that are studying you. Not benignly, but with a judgemental interest. Hundreds and hundreds of Englishmen sitting on a court-martial of beefy genius. There isn't an English face as such, and this is not a beautiful or noble race, but they do have a common look. It's in their expression and they've passed it on, one to the other, from one generation to the next. It's a portentous blankness, a masterly inactivity.

3

Voice

At the start of the Taliban/Afghan war I was in Peshawar on the North-West Frontier, a trading city at the foot of the Khyber Pass. Here the sub-continental Grand Trunk Road made magic by Kipling in *Kim* goes up the high passes and valleys of Afghanistan before meeting the Silk Route in Central Asia. This is a crossroads of the oldest trading network in the world, a gateway for invasion and a mud-brick warren of kidnap and vendetta. Peshawar has been a haven for soldiers, dealers, traders, smugglers, thieves, secret agents, policemen, dacoits, mercenaries, revolutionaries, refugees, the lost, the hiding and the hopeless, for thousands of years. There are a dozen languages and a hundred dialects spoken here.

With the approaching war it was full of Pathans who had struggled across the border to escape being bombed. This is where the *mujahidin* came to rest and make plans, and it has the largest free-for-all arms market in the East. It's a major depot for opium, stolen cars and counterfeit everything, from Marks and Spencer's pullovers to Kylie CDs.

The frontier is usually described as lawless, but it's quite the reverse. It has far too much law, a great deal of it contradictory and much of it extempore. I was walking through a dark and crowded market and turned a corner into a narrow alley that was a dead end. Sitting in a little open shop were a group of young men. They were dressed in the hats and shawls of the Pathan and didn't seem to be selling or buying anything, and I sensed that

I'd stumbled into something I'd have been better out of. So I made my *salaam* and touched my chest with my right hand. The bearded dark men watched me under their brows without replying, and very slowly one of them stood up and took a step towards me. 'You lost, mate?' he said, and I laughed. I laughed because he said it in an unmistakably thick Midlands accent. I laughed because a Birmingham accent is funny. You can't help it. It's stupid and in this case plain wrong. There was nothing funny about this handful of British Pakistani boys who'd come back here to fight. They were far more potentially frightening than the local *jihadis*. Familiarity with me and my type would have bred more than mere contempt. But that sing-song voice flicked a switch on a lifetime of metropolitan prejudice. It overrode the setting and the clothes, the politics and common-sense. I laughed. And he told me to go back where I'd come from and turn left, and we wished each other luck.

Mark Tully, the BBC foreign correspondent, used to rail at broadcasting's reluctance to put Indians on the news. Producers would drop interviews or vox pops and apologize, with crisp BBC accents, that Indians all sounded like Peter Sellers. Britain has over 200 identifiable accents, probably more than any comparable country. English, outside Britain, has hundreds more, and every single one of them makes someone else laugh – or wince, or scowl.

Accent is the last great redoubt of prejudice. The race relations industry, that inquisition of fairness and sensitivity, doesn't protect against discrimination by funny voice. You can mock an accent with impunity, and everyone does. Call centres won't use West Country accents because they sound slow and gullible; Irish is charming but not trustworthy; Yorkshire is the most popular accent for commercials because it sounds both guileless and friendly, but next-door Lancashire is hard and nagging. Scots is popular for telling people things, as it sounds intelligent, while Welsh and Scouse sound like whingeing lies. Cockney is dodgy but funny, East Anglian spooky and inbred. I should admit here that I am speaking to you with what is sometimes called BBC English or RP, Received Pronunciation. For a Scot, it's not a great sound. It's English English. And I know Scots who simply won't accept that someone who sounds like me could be Scottish at all. This voice betrays the soul of a Sassenach. People who sound Italian or Punjabi can be as Scots as haggis, but not those who sound English.

No one really knows why England has made up so many accents, why there are so many small tribes that needed to be identified by sound. Is this really such a sectarian nation that it has to tag a native for life by the sound of their voice? Accent and pronunciation are a never-ending source of subtle snobbery and fury for the English. Regional accents grow out of geography and history and trade. Lancashire is spoken with a tight mouth because of bad industrial air and the snow of cotton dross; Geordie singsongs like Scandinavian, a verbal memory of the Viking; on the other side of the country, Liverpudlian owes much of its roundness to the Irish, and Ulster-Irish sounds like Glasgow-Scots, and West Country-Scots sounds like Southern Irish.

On top of all this, overlying it, is the noise that I make, this Received Pronunciation. It's an accent that's widely thought not to be an accent at all, but the default note of spoken English, a *correct* pronunciation – as if all the other ways of speaking were more or less incorrect. RP doesn't come from any region or job and it doesn't have a history, although it's more associated with the south than the north. It is the voice of authority. The sound of the professions.

An American man from Boston has a Boston accent. He has it whether he sells hot dogs or is a Kennedy. Regional accents in America are regional from top to bottom, though they may be stronger or thicker in working-class mouths, but essentially you speak the same as everyone around you. Not so the English.

Received Pronunciation is an accent that comes with an added layer of assumption about education, aesthetics, jobs, money, housing, holidays, politics, your shoes, your car, your pastimes and appetites and your potential power. I once asked a Highland Brigade sergeant how he could tell an officer in the dark. 'He'll sound like an Englishman,' he replied, then without a beat added: 'He'll sound like you.'

The term Received Pronunciation isn't some phonetician's technical term; it comes from Nancy Mitford, who wrote in an arch-whimsical way about manners that started as a drawing-room amusement and ended up as a behavioural manual. She referred to a pronunciation that was fit to be received into society, and this nasty, sniggering little snobbery slipped neatly into the language as an appropriate term for my voice. But how come the English ever needed a separate business-class accent?

Firstly, it is simple snobbery, and we all know the English love a bit of a distinction. As a young man I did all sorts of blue-collar work – gardening decorating, working in warehouses, shops and building sites, and in every one my voice was a constant source of teasing. It was assumed that I would be able to do crossword clues, that I could arbitrate arguments on points of geography, history and culture. My voice predicted that I'd be useless in a fight and wouldn't know how to drink properly, that I'd be a good flirt but a lousy shag – all this gleaned from no other information other than the way I said 'bath' and 'trousers'. It was also assumed that I didn't belong in the manual world, that I was a failure or misdirected. Men I worked with would often take me aside and ask what I was doing in a job like this. They'd shake their heads and say that I should be doing better, that I must be a worry to me mum. I pointed out to one boy that we were the same age – he had more qualifications than me and we were doing the same job for the same money. So how come I was the failure and he was the success? 'Get off it,' he said, in a south London accent, 'you know we're not the same.'

In almost every particular we were. We lived in the same sort of bedsit, drank in the same boozer, ate the same food, got lucky with the same girls, played pool, told the same jokes, but I spoke my way and he spoke his. It wasn't simply the sound of white-collar management, it was also the accepted sound of getting on fast tracks and into executive lounges and preferential treatment.

At about the same time, I had a conversation with a magistrate who said quite candidly that 'if a boy with a nice [her word] accent appeared in the dock I would be more willing to think of his crime as a youthful mistake, as high spirits, and give him a second chance. I know this all seems horribly class-ridden and probably quite shocking to you, but that's because you don't see the cases I see. I know that a boy with a nice voice is likely to have a family that will support him and take him in hand, that his prospects are good or better, and I wouldn't want to ruin them with a criminal conviction. We don't serve the community by cutting off the careers of those who'll do the most to serve it.' And you can read the future from an accent? I asked. She rolled her eyes to imply that I was now being wilfully dim. 'Of course you can. You and I both know that. A magistrate meets the world as it is, not as you'd like it to be. I can't even claim to be making society better, I just try and stop it getting worse, and an accent is an indicator of future behaviour and achievement.' But, I asked, don't you think that this may just be a self-fulfilling truism? If you treat people who sound like me preferentially, then of course they will get on. 'Yes, that may well be true, but society has to be organized some way. You work it out. You're a smart boy, you've got a nice voice.'

I remember this conversation so clearly even though it took place over thirty years ago, because it made me so angry. It was the utter belief of the magistrate. She wasn't just being correct, but humane. She believed that accent was an indicator of goodness in the way that a fundamental Catholic believes in the odour of sanctity. She knew there was the sound of rightness and her experience of life confirmed it and her actions buttressed it. It was the sweetness, the reason, the care and the concern that were so shocking. It was a very English position, cloaking prejudice and wishful thinking.

This is an English type that is familiar to anyone who has lived here for a couple of years. A person of quiet rectitude, of great personal kindness, who cares for their community, taking part in the dull but necessary running of things, sitting in church, taking books to hospitals, forming Neighbourhood Watches, organizing lifts for children and the elderly, lobbying for pedestrian crossings and the protection of flowers. But amidst all this is hidden a monstrous prejudice, a really repellent blanket of cancer, a gin trap set in a herbaceous border.

Received Pronunciation isn't just the sound of authority and privilege, it's also the resonant interval mutter of the culture, the arts. It's the voice of the audio guide to an exhibition, the commentary on the documentary, the voice of auctioneers and curators, or bibliophiles and antiquarians. Actors used to go to diction classes to bury their regional accents. They laugh at that now. Drama schools support and nurture vocal diversity and television goes out of its way not to sound so iconically BBC, but this only underlines the dominance of RP. Actors who only speak with Geordie accents only get parts with Geordie accents. You could work in British film and theatre and TV without ever having to speak Ulster Irish or Devonian, but you'd be severely limiting your employment opportunities if you couldn't speak like the officer/managerial class. Quite apart from anything else, it has the biggest back catalogue.

RP is the sound of classic novels. When you read poetry to yourself it's the accent in your head. We think we know that Byron sounded like this, and Donne and Shakespeare, and no amount of literary historians or phonetic archaeologists telling you that Shakespeare had a Birmingham accent (or whatever pre-industrial Warwickshire sounded like) is going to make him sound any less like a World Service announcer. It couldn't matter less that Shakespeare is more likely to have sounded like a Punjabi engineer than to have spoken Received Pronunciation.

RP is the interior cadence of the Book of Common Prayer and the great King James Bible, based on translations by Tyndale and a committee of bishops who must all have had regional accents as bright and dissonant as a patchwork quilt, but it's come down to us as the voice of a civil deity. And most important of all is that RP is the voice of the dictionary. It is the arbiter of what is and isn't correct. Those small squiggles and reverse letters that are the musical annotation of language direct your tongue towards RP.

And for some that will be natural, but for others, for most of us, it's like putting on a funny voice. This amounts to a sort of verbal apartheid. When you write dialogue or recorded speech it's completely beyond the pale to couch it phonetically in the way that Kipling or Dickens did. You simply can't write 'Oi tink oim far hit' as music hall Irish or 'werrily werrily young master' as East End Jewish, it's too liberally patronizing and most editors simply wouldn't print it any more than they would print Mick or Yid. So to indicate an accent you have to stipulate it. 'Good morning,' she said, in a soft West Highland brogue, but you never have to write 'Good morning,' she said in Received Pronunciation. The written word is already Received Pronunciation. It forces words into particular combinations and favours some sounds over others, and by its nature makes the language strong in areas that suit it.

RP is not, however, the voice of the traditional ruling class or the aristocracy, a dry drawl which is pretty much extinct now. Nobody would want to be caught with it in their mouths. It makes you laugh, it's the voice of people who have nothing to say, because they don't have to say anything. Being interesting and chatty is what people without acres and horses do. An ageless ticking silence is the preferred noise of the English aristocracy, their reedy voices never exactly rang across the land and have now vanished, except in a very few affected mouths.

If you listen to recordings of the Queen when she was a young girl during the war she has the unmistakable call of her class. Then listen to her opening Parliament last year, and you'll hear that she has dropped into the safe and reassuring tone of the managerial class. She now speaks RP. Prince Philip still favours Old Aristo, but we don't really know whether that's because he doesn't listen to anyone else or because he knows it's irritating. The Queen has moved her voice to be more in line with her most supportive subjects.

What is it that made this rootless new bland accent so successful? You might see it as a piece of social Darwinism. All organisms look for environmental opportunities to exploit. The old geographic accents naturally made sense for groups who lived and worked in the place they were born. It made them cohesive and it was easy to identify strangers. But during the eighteenth century England became a country on the move. The Industrial Revolution and a series of agricultural collapses pushed people into cities and the conurbations of new industry, where a thick local accent would have gone from being a protection to a liability.

The growing salesman, clerking and briefcase professions needed a new voice; and their children, who would run the empire and oversee the trade that was its purpose, were sent to the burgeoning boarding schools, where a regional accent would be a terrible hazard (as indeed it still can be). Quick as a mocking trice kids learnt to speak proper, to talk nice and grow red-eared with embarrassment at the sound of their parents. Received Pronunciation moved from mouth to mouth, a loquacious, adaptable, eloquent, slippery tongue. It was the noise of the middle class and it went on to colonize the culture, the arts, the theatre, the middle-brow novel, academia, medicine, banking, the law, and with that lot under its lip it pretty much had control of everything.

Received Pronunciation gave its new owner an edge, a leg-up. That little Darwinian advantage. Employers who spoke that way would want their offices filled with others who spoke like them, but they wouldn't have wanted it on the shop floor, where it sounds mocking. It gives you the edge in a magistrates' court and gets a polite response from a doorman or policeman and, in true survival-of-the-fittest terms, Received Pronunciation seeks out its own and protects its niche. It fights off other accents, placing traps of pronunciation, making pariahs of apparently blameless words. Nancy Mitford, who gave it its name, also made a game of mockery. The way others spoke, the knowing smirk, at meal and pardon, mirror and mantelpiece, toilet and serviette. Sometimes words simply *volte-face* to catch out the *parvenu*. You notice I've used a pair of foreign phrases there. This was very chic amongst the Edwardians. The years between the death of Victoria and the Great War were possibly the most socially insecure since the Elizabethans. Etiquette, manners and language accrued a low liturgical importance and the aspirant middle classes took to peppering their conversations with Italian and French phrases, where a generation before it might have been Latin or Greek. This implied not just a private education, but that the user was well travelled. So words like serviette, mirror and toilet were very soigné, and then *naturellement* servants began using the same words, which instantly tarnished their chic and made them common; they became solecisms that mothers would blush and hiss at when they were brought home from school by innocent and confused infants. That was until about fifteen years ago. Then there was a smart demi-trend. To use the word toilet but with a hint of a charlady accent. This implied that you were a young lady of the world and a democratic egalitarian and that you were using the wrong word on purpose as an act of mad-cap daring.

Other things that were often considered common were abbreviations, like phone and bus and cab, but then that was overturned by Sloane Hoorays who used military and girls' school abbreviations. My favourite was from a girl I once collected to take to a party. I waited in her minute living-room surrounded by the huddled ranks of family photographs, always a feature of Sloane digs, and as she passed one gloomy-looking gent she said with precise cadence, 'That's daddy. He committed suir.'

The mechanics of Received Pronunciation are fascinating. What lies under the tongue, why it's been the most successful of all English accents.

To begin with, it's spoken in iambic pentameter, five beats to a line. Iambic verse was originally dedicated to the cult of Demeter and was often satirical or mocking. When Demeter went to mourn the loss of Persephone in the Underworld, she was made to laugh at a joke told by Iambe, which seemed particularly fitting to the English – giggling at your daughter's abduction by a filthy old man who lives underground.

Iambic pentameter is the beat of Shakespeare. It's emphatic and memorable. It's the beat of oratory and statement rather than enquiry and conversation, and it's perfect for the passing of instruction or orders. Received Pronunciation hits the black notes. It's in a major key, which is the sound of assurance and confidence. A Birmingham accent is in a minor key, and a minor key sounds querulous and questioning. Iambic pentameter stresses information, and in RP the beat lands on the consonants. Stressing consonants imparts fact, but hides emotion. In American English, the emphasis is on the vowel. Vowels are where the emotion of language lives. Opera, for example, is all vowels, all emotion.

American accents sound more emotionally honest and open than BBC English, which uses pitch to stress meaning. It goes up and down a lot. American English uses volume, and gets louder the more emphatic it becomes. Received Pronunciation is a perfect accent for giving orders and lecturing. It utilizes all the verbal tools for implying confidence; it has natural authority and sounds like the facts. What it doesn't sound like is the truth. It's designed specifically to mask emotion. You have a Darwinian Machiavellian choice – the noise you make can earn you respect or love. Both have a social value and drawbacks. The middle-class English chose respect. In an insecure mobile social stratum, respect is what you aim for, respect is a marketable commodity, respect is dependable and solid. It's money in the bank. Love is a soft, fickle luxury and an extravagance. Received English is one of the least physically demonstrative languages in the world. It doesn't use hand gestures or facial expression in the way that other European languages do. It doesn't show its teeth and it doesn't lend itself to eye contact. English has such a capacious and adaptable vocabulary, but no secondary language skills, with a semaphore or girning. The assumption is that these are strap-ons for insufficient paupers' dictionaries, that a gesture is simple frustration at not having the right word, that the ideal model of communication is two Englishmen talking to each other with their heads averted and their hands in their pockets. A broadside of two great dreadnoughts aiming salvoes of fact and observation at each other in gossamer-fine gradations of meaning, probably about something of very little consequence. Rose-growing, or civil administration in the Sudan.

There is of course another explanation for why the English don't like gestures. Non-verbal and facial communication are older than spoken language by a few million years. We are all instinctively trained to read them before we can speak. We have a greater sensitivity to faces and gestures than to words. It's always very difficult to lie with your face and your hands. So the less you use them, the less you give away.

If you watch American films with the sound turned off, you can usually tell what's happening. The story's readable through body-language. Often you can understand quite complex plots and emotions without hearing what anyone's saying. But with an English film, it's almost always impossible. There is barely any indication of what the participants are thinking or talking about. The most extreme example is *Brief Encounter*, David Lean's melodrama of thwarted love between the characters played by Trevor Howard and Celia Johnson. This is a story of the highest emotion, but turn the sound down and you'd never know. In fact the characters' reserve is so complete that they're utterly English. Even when you can hear what they say, the emotion has to be carried by the Rachmaninov score. It needed a Russian romantic to add the love. So the upwardly peripatetic English middle class invented an accent that was precise, rhythmic, plausible, confident, learned and authoritative. But it was also emotionally obtuse and truncated. It was the perfect tool for academics, lawyers, businessmen, novelists, playwrights, poets, politicians, doctors, civil servants, salesmen, estate agents, wine merchants, auctioneers, lotharios, wife beaters, bigamists, bankrupts, moral inadequates, cowards, bores and the most mendacious, po-faced, perfidious, righteous liars in the world.

The constant question about all language is: 'Do people fashion the tongue or does the tongue make the people?' Received Pronunciation is such a snug mask for the English, such a neatly bespoke accent. Yet it has the ability to be moulded and to subtly change. The very clipped and staccato delivery of Celia Johnson has become rounder and slower, the edges less polished, but it is still audibly the same major-key iambic pentameter thumping the consonants, and can accommodate the occasional twang of other accents, the northern flat vowel, an Asian flourish. There is a suspicion that RP proscribes some thoughts, that it gently moulds the characters of those who choose to talk with it, that if you speak like a middle-class Englishman, sooner or later you will think like one and have become one. Received Pronunciation is the accent that foreigners aim to imitate when they learn English, but it is also the second accent of more British people than any other. Very few Geordies train their voices to Somerset, and hardly any Yorkshiremen work on speaking Brummie, but thousands learn to speak or allow themselves to slip into Received Pronunciation and they encourage their children to do so. It's probably the only accent in the English-speaking world where parents will correct their children's pronunciation as if it were good and bad manners. Speaking Received Pronunciation English is status and an achievement. Even before you've said anything interesting.

The Queen may have mutated her accent from strangulated toff to urban middle class, but her grandchildren have taken their glottal stops further downmarket and talk in an accent that is sometimes called mockney when public schoolboys use it, but it's better known as Estuary. An accent that is flat, unimaginative, diluted Cockney. It has spread across the country from the London over-spill of the Thames Estuary and the Essex Marshes. It's an accent that slurs where RP is crisp. It elides and swallows consonants. It's in a minor key and it sounds nasal, whiney and dishonest. It uses the quiff of American and Australian rhythms to raise up the ends of sentences, so everything sounds like a rhetorical question. Estuary is fast becoming the English noise. Colonizing other accents, inflections of Estuary can now be heard as far west as Taunton, and it's making its way through Birmingham and has even been heard as far north as Liverpool. It travels via the young. There is nothing cool about being sixteen and sounding like a character from *Tess of the D'Urbervilles*. The pressure on teenagers to ditch the rural drawl, like everything about being a teenager, is compelling. There are many reasons for welcoming the final adoption of a classless, pan-national accent. It would once and for all do away with Shavian snobbery and silence the last great cause of prejudice and distinction.

Of course, nothing raises so much ire amongst the English as Estuary. It's aesthetically unpleasant, it lacks gravitas, philosophy or nobility. The Japanese have a word for an onomatopoeia that seems to catch the essence of an action or a thing. There's nothing like it in English. The closest might be a word like waddle, which seems to have in it the spirit of the description. Estuary has in its sound the spirit and essence of the people who use it. It has a propensity to limited and repetitive vocabulary and uses meaningless words as punctuation: 'yeah', 'innit', 'like'. It creates an oral picture of the lives and attitudes of the people who sound like this as slovenly, feckless, cowardly, vicious, thick, cunning, opportunistic, demanding, overly entitled, emotionally blunted, compulsively eroticized, tarty, shag-stinking, lying scum. Estuary is the dark side of RP. It is equally bereft of emotional colour and just as insouciant. It serves as a marvellously satisfying assault course for the huge and energetic platoons of middle-mouthed, angry Englishmen. Medium-incomed, medium-educated, maximum-irked English can go lickity-spittle over the vileness of Estuary Pronunciation. It can fill their cheeks with the nuts of lazy pronunciation. They can do karaoke impressions of common children and laugh with a hangman's pleasure at the irredeemable, damnable sound and content of Estuary. It is just another of the cul-de-sacs for English anger. There is nowhere for it to go. Being furious with the way people sound is as pointless as being furious about their height. But in the Angry Island it serves a laudable purpose of being a safe place to dump those ever-present psychopathically murderous feelings. You can bite and chew and grind at an accent for ever. Rip it to shreds, ridicule it, but it makes not the slightest difference. Estuary goes on oblivious, unscathed.

It is a voice that lends itself to a whole raft of modern professions that RP simply can't manage without sounding pretentious or ridiculous: disc jockey, reality TV presenter, bouncer, computer geek, personal trainer, property spiv, chef, model agent, pop manager, celebrity PR. Estuary is a mongrel mouth. It can accommodate immigrant accents and syntax. It's hungry for pidgin words and mutant meanings. As RP lends itself to certain modes and thoughts and encourages particular subjects and vocabulary, so Estuary inhabits its own quarter of concern as a collective accent. And where RP favours a lecture, a seminar or a Platonic conversation, Estuary is extemplore. It's the voice of mob enthusiasm. It's much happier at sustained bellowing over the jukebox, the plasma surround-sound. It sounds good in crowds. RP sounds shrill and desperate when it raises its voice. It is by nature solitary, self-conscious and controlled. Estuary clings to other voices, making competitive choirs of noise. It's an accent with the rising and falling rhythm that's geared for telling jokes. It has an in-built inflection of humour and teasing. It's the accent of first-name sex. You can talk dirty, hiss breathless body instructions, plead and exhort in Estuary where you just couldn't in BBC English. Most of us afflicted with RP accents fornicate in muscled silence, occasionally passing notes to each other. Nothing shrivels the moment or paralyses the erogenous atmosphere like a Benenden voice offering encouragement and direction. Estuary is the accent of Friday nights and stag nights and laughing in the dark with your mates. It's the sound of having a giggle, taking the piss, having fun. And that was something RP never managed. I've always been aware of how bad my voice is at doing enthusiasm, or spontaneity, or exuberance. Trained for understatement and reserve, modulated for instruction and summing up, it misses out on letting rip or being daft as a loon. It's not that people like me don't want to sound like slappers on a Saturday night out in a pedestrian precinct, it's that our mouths won't let us out. We sound stupid at football matches and we're shit at jokes. RP is the voice that asks for respect, Estuary asks for friendship.

In a generation there are likely to be only two accents left in England. Mine and Estuary. They will collide, then elide into each other so that our mouths will be able to slip from the boardroom to the call centre, from the common-room to the pub, the dress circle to the terraces. If you had to do one thing that would improve the collective life of England without having to spend a penny or pass a law, it would be to invent a single English voice where you could sound Oxford at dinner and Chelmsford in bed.

4

Memorials

Go to Paddington Station to platform one and you'll see a man reading a letter. He's always there. Stare at him for a bit. He's there to be stared at. And if you don't feel a pricking in the corner of your eye, or a nut of emotion in your gullet, you're made of sterner stuff than me, though not him.

On the fourth anniversary of the end of the Great War, 'Soldier reading a letter' – bronze standing on black marble and Mezzano white marble, Aberdeen grey and Belgian black granite – was unveiled by the Board of the Great Western Railway in remembrance of the 3,312 men and women of the company who gave their lives for King, country and that complicated and spectral coalition of politics and emotion that was the enigmatic motivation for the war that began the modern age.

The soldier was sculpted by Charles Sargeant Jagger, who produced two of the greatest war memorials made. This is one of them. The soldier stands waiting for a train, his helmet set at an angle, his greatcoat slung over his shoulder, the collar turned up. He's wearing the muffler his mother knitted for him, and he's looking down at a letter. He holds it gently, saving the envelope – it will have to sustain many readings. His face shows no outward emotion, it has that concentrated calm we use for letters and hymn sheets, and standing for the two minutes' silence. His feet are firmly placed on his plinth, he has a purposeful air. Just now he's reading and waiting for his train, but soon he'll get down to business, soon he'll be dead. But now, he stands here on platform one, an immortal everybody in bronze, waiting and re-reading his letter. The eye is constantly drawn to the letter, the lines and the tensions of the sculpture tug you back; it's been folded in the old-fashioned way, like a pamphlet for people who are frugal with notepaper.

Letters from and to soldiers are so familiar to us; they are the stuff of drama and war films, of sadness and of memorized poetry. The letters of war are great symbols of national empathy, particularly for the English, who like to think of themselves as, if not people of letters, then the children of people of letters. And as a nation that's chronically incapable of expressing emotion, and even proud of this constipated inability, the letter is a stiff-lipped device for imparting something that you really wanted to say, but hadn't managed to. Except that not being able to say it in letters is also a particularly English trait. Reading between the lines is England's second language, and perhaps that's appropriate for a railway station.

It's the little strained observations of life that are so chest-tighteningly poignant. The small, bland, uncomfortable stabs at intimacy, the heavy metaphor of trivia and understatement. 'Hoping this finds you as it leaves me,' 'Chin up', 'No sense in grumbling', 'All the best', 'Remember me to . . . remember me'. We know all the small plots of war letters, and we wonder who this one is from – a mother's note that came with the scarf, and a tin of cigarettes from a sweetheart, this being the age before girlfriends; good luck from workmates, a wife perhaps? Though he's young to be married, but then they were, weren't they? Too young for any of it.

As you stare at the young man reading his letter, you grow too hot to blush and realize that actually, of course, it's from you. You're composing it as you look at him, at this bronze boy who reads the thing you wanted to say, but were never able to. How England went on without him, how the station's changed, he'd not recognize half the stuff in the coffee shop, the tea's still dreadful but hot and sweet, that his country still thinks about him. And the great-grandchildren with the names he'd hear as strange – not a Wilf, Alf or Herbert amongst them – send their best and hope this finds you as it leaves us. Thank you.

This was not Jagger's first idea for the memorial of the Great Western Railway. At first he proposed a soldier carrying a trench catapult – he liked kit, he knew what it was for and what it did. He knew that soldiers had become extensions of things, of stuff – fuel for the machine. The Memorial Committee was chaired by Winston Churchill and he was a man who knew the truth of the English heart, the image that gripped their shy sense of belonging. He asked Jagger to think again, and the soldier with the letter was born out of the clay that his inspiration had dug, blown up and finally been buried in. It always seems an almost unbearable irony that these memorials start with mud and grow to become molten, then cold metal – a transubstantiation that is life and death and resurrection and immortality.

War memorials are the great blessing of the English. Culturally, they are their finest creation. In every village stands the Mons cross with the sword, the white stone and the list of names: the repetition of brothers, the bucolic-whispered rhythm of the long-disbanded regiments, the salty names of up-ended ships, the litany of extinct countries, the dedication of brick village halls, the familiar phrases: 'Known only to God', 'Men of this village – this town, this county'. There are the marble lists on shop stairwells, in stations, drapers and haberdashers, the names of tweenies and skivvies and draymen, and then the later additions from the Second World War, the same names back again. Over time war memorials grow in stature, they don't grow old as other art grows old. Their simplicity and honesty, their grave purpose and their heavy mordant elegance grows into the age. They seem to anticipate the look of things to come, the brutal, minimal stark lines and planes, the emptiness of the post-war world.

The war memorials of the English are one of the half dozen single greatest national collections of cultural artefacts from the last explosively creative century. That's not hyperbole, it's not said to be provocative, but war memorials contain a power that few made objects ever achieve. They're public, they're created with the highest aspirations, but they are instantly comprehensible to everyone who sees them. They are both literal and metaphorical, poetic and functional. War memorials are a focal point in communities, familiar without ever being banal. And it isn't that they piggy-back on solemnity or emotion; most foreign war memorials fail, fail disastrously, drowning in soups of bathos and operatic sorrow. No other country in the world has come close to achieving the synthesis of subject and object that the English managed at the end of the Great War.

Imagine Jagger's soldier on a French plinth. He would have been clutching his heart, looking at heaven. French war memorials reek of music-hall sentimentality, the hackneyed glory of the dead, the histrionic sacrifice, the public display of righteous hysteria. They're sad for all the wrong reasons. German war memorials have all the double-speak problems of being memorials to both the victims and the accused. Memorializing murderers is tricky, so they concentrate on weeping mothers with big hands. The Russians went for corporate gigantism – the size is impressive, but they lack emotion, are purposefully impersonal. All Russian brides used to go straight from their secular marriage-solemnizing rooms to lay their bouquets on the nearest war memorial. You see these little posies lying under the caterpillar tracks of preserved tanks. Stoic, impressive, determined but not moving poppies. The English worked very, very hard at getting war memorials right. Almost as soon as the eleventh hour of the eleventh day of the eleventh month had chimed, they were setting up committees and working parties and advisory boards to find fitting images. If they couldn't quite make a land fit for heroes, then they'd do their damnedest to make memorials fit for the dead.

No country, no artist, had ever been confronted with a commission like the Great War. It's almost inconceivable to encompass the freshness of the sorrow, the vastness of the death and the exhausted relief that shrouded England like mist. But England was lucky to have a group of artists – and in particular architects – who rose to a moment with a collective vision. It was almost sublime. Edwin Lutyens, the architect who designed the Viceroy's Palace in Delhi and made beautiful solicitors' country houses, created the Cenotaph in Whitehall. It was made first in wood and plaster for the memorial day of 1919, but a year later it was replaced by Portland stone. With the simple inscription: 'The glorious dead' written by Kipling, who had lost his only son at the Battle of Loos. He was almost entombed in grief and guilt at his own role in recruiting young men for what he grew to believe was a corrupt waste of so many lives. He wrote impotent, raging epitaphs for imaginary graves and his longest book, which no one now reads, is the regimental history of the Irish Guards, the Grey Geese. When it comes to the page where Second Lieutenant Jack Kipling is killed he's simply written in the list of missing, along with a few others who perished that day. Kipling didn't allow himself a single word, comma or pause of emotion. What a labour of love, what an English act of gratuitous sublimation. Whatever his private feelings, he came up with exactly the correct understatement for the Cenotaph.

The obvious references for memorials were classical. Most of England and its Empire was decoratively modelled on Greece via Rome, and the look of much memorial furniture owes its proportions and starkness to the antique. But there are hints of other cultures too. In Lutyens's simple pedestal plinth and basilicas there is something noble; there is also an echo, a nod to the Anglican Church and the shadowy halls of public schools, and in the Cenotaph's look there are more ancient memories of standing stones and henges, the birthstones of England. The Cenotaph, with its simple lines, its quiet solemnity in the middle of the bustle of the street of Government, where the taxis and the delivery vans and the lost tourists trundle round it, is like a cliff of stillness in the din. It's a perfect evocation of grief and pride. Its proportions are deeply pleasing, an imperceptible balm. There is no extraneous decoration to snag your eye, no graphic image to make your thoughts specific, no gratuitous outburst, no protestations of hereafter or eternity, no false promise of immortality or a better place, nor, most admirably, most typically, not an ounce, a hint of triumphalism. There are just carved stone wreaths. The simplicity and stillness of the stone is contrasted by the standards, the flags that drape themselves, with the folds of shrouds hiding their brightness. The colours are where soldiers go to muster, to rally, to make a stand and finally drape their coffins; the Cenotaph has to be the focus of a nation's martial remembrance, but every individual must be able to come with their personal memories of grief and gratitude – all faiths and none. Every emotion must be equally welcome, everyone needs to be able to stare and see what they need; and who can now imagine the fathoms of emotion, the blessings and curses poured on the Cenotaph in that first November of 1920. It is a faultless piece of design. How daunting the task of finding a silent thing that can eloquently imply the unsayable.

Lutyens was busy with memorials. In particular, the great gate at Thiepval, remembering the dead without graves. He was also asked to design another memorial for the Royal Artillery at Hyde Park Corner. There had been lengthy negotiations for a suitable site. He offered a number of architectural schemes which were rejected, mostly on the grounds that they were too large for the surrounding buildings and weren't specific enough to the gunners. He submitted more drawings, along with the sculptor Derwent Wood, but the committee were still not happy with the scale or the focus and they asked Jagger to submit a design. He envisaged a howitzer on a plinth, like a gun emplacement with four bronze gunners on each face. After much disagreement and modification, including the queries of the King who would have to ride past it every morning on his constitutional, the design was agreed.

Originally the gun was to face north over Hyde Park. Lutyens, who was still involved with the committee, suggested moving it around to face south so that its elevation balanced the natural rise of the land. Jagger agreed and set to work on what would be the most evocatively emotive and terribly beautiful war memorial, and one of the best public statues anywhere.

Jagger himself had just returned from serving in the war. He had been awarded the Prix de Rome, a year-long scholarship to study in Italy, the year war was declared, and he immediately joined up. But the bursary was still paid to him out of the pockets of older sculptors, because they felt that he and the other young men were doing the correct thing. He joined the Artists' Rifles, which acted as a clearing house for officers to other regiments. He was sent to Suvla Bay, Gallipoli, as Second Lieutenant in the Worcesters. The three men he shared a cabin with on the voyage out were all killed. One, Douglas Greenway, he wrote, had died like an English gentleman performing an act of unselfish gallantry, bringing in the wounded from no-man's-land. Jagger was haunted by Greenway's death and the awful conditions on that stony beach. He was wounded in the shoulder and sent home and then back to France, where, in 1918, he defended an exposed position with fifty men and little ammunition until relief came. He continued to fight until he was shot through the lung by a machine gun, and for this he was awarded the Military Cross.

It is a grim but obvious truth that after a war is a good time to be a sculptor. Jagger was also working-class and straight-talking from the north, and that must have helped. But what helped most was that Jagger knew from first-hand what it was he was sculpting, and what it meant. Rarely for a war artist, he knew what war felt like and he had a soldier's obsession with kit.

I once did a story on snipers in the British Army; all they talked about was their equipment, their boots, sleeping-bag, coats, knives, guns, goggles, water-bottle. Any one thing can be the difference between you making it and nearly making it, between lying awake in the freezing wet and sleeping in the warm. You can feel this in Jagger's soldiers; they aren't immortal heroes, personifications of sacrifice and bravery draped in human clothing like fancy dress or chiffon – their clothes and accoutrements cover them like armour. They pull their coats on against the weather and their pockets bulge; there is weight and texture to this stuff of war. Everything works; the buckles, the buttons, the straps and badges all mean something practical.

The soldiers on the south, east and west of the monument are defined by the tools of their calling: the shell-carrier has heavy panniers slung from his shoulders; the officer carries his great-coat and is slung with binoculars, gas mask and Sam Browne; the driver from the Royal Horse Artillery leans back against the emplacement in his rain-cape, whip in hand, the leather gaiter on his right leg because he rides the left-hand horse on the gun team. War for the men who have to fight it is a practical business, a job with tools, mechanical frustrations and satisfactions. Their faces are square-jawed, tough and resolute; not fretful or urgent or placidly ethereal; they're not thinking metaphysics.

They would like to put aside the heavy load of shells and capes and tin hats and Sam Brownes and put on other clothes as mechanics and ploughmen and dockers, miners and teachers. They'd like to have looked determined and purposeful doing something else, but for now they'll see to this. Jaggers' men are always citizen soldiers, not in the dry, classical, public school Athenian sense, but in a new twentieth-century way. The men are made competent and powerful by their mastery of the machine. These aren't Englishmen offering their lives as sacrifice, these are blokes sent to do a nasty job as best they can, whose heroism comes from their hands, not from Latin tags and snippets of Horace in their heads.

The figure on the north side is quite different. You only know he's present because of his equipment. He's dead. Covered by a greatcoat. There was a great deal of committee discussion about this figure, objections that it was distressing, that it was too low and might suffer indignity. But what is really disturbing is that it breaks a convention of war memorials, whose implication is that the dead live again, in a better place, a Valhalla, Elysian Fields, or at least the cricket pitch at Eton. Here is a dead man unrisen; he hasn't stepped over to the pantheon of the immortal. There is an enormous pathos in the figure, the weight and fall of the greatcoat, the turn of his feet, the puttees and heavy boots at rest. It's a figure of terrible sadness and pride, evoking the tombs of Norman crusaders in cathedrals. But he's not one of them, he's not a champion but a common soldier, a gunner. Beneath him is written a 'Royal Fellowship of Death', a quote from *Henry V*.

When the memorial was finally unveiled by the Duke of Connaught it provoked vicious criticism for its size, its realism, its dead body and its gun. The 9.2 howitzer is life-size, realized in stone, raised above the classical metaphor and harmony of Hyde Park. 'A hideous fire-spitting toad', it was called. The anger was directed at the depiction of the machines of war. The gun had committed such carnage. This was the mincing-machine that churned up the gallant and the coward alike, that reduced glory to mathematics, engineering and chemistry. The howitzer is a masterful and brilliant image to place on this catafalque of the first modern war.

Artillery regiments don't have colours like the infantry or cavalry; gunners rally to their guns. To lose a gun is like losing the standard, except that here, high up, it is a point for their final stand. It's a strikingly twentieth-century motif, the awe-some power of mechanics and science. Traditionally, some High Church symbol with wings would have stood here, but this gun of metal made stone with its nose of smoke is set to launch a salvo at heaven, or perhaps just to flatten Victoria Station.

It's not just the memorial to the gunners, it's a message *from* the gunners. The Royal Artillery loved it. They wrote a touching letter to Jagger saying that he had almost become part of the regiment. This memorial has grown in stature over the genera-tions, becoming a statue for our age, the age of common men and machines. If generals are always doomed to fight the last war, then retired generals on committees always seem to want to memorialize an imaginary war of a thousand years ago. Look at what surrounds the artillery memorial at Hyde Park Corner – at the centre of the roundabout is the great Arch, which once contained the smallest police station in London. On top of it is the quadriga, a chariot carrying the winged victory or Nike, the Goddess of Victories. Beneath her there's the Duke of Wellington on a horse on a plinth, surrounded by bored-looking Napoleonic soldiers dressed up in the parade pomp that is the obsession of military fashion victims and toy-soldier collectors Wellington always looked so uninspiring in his bronze outing, and there are enough of them. A man who despised the Army, hated soldiers and was cynically understated about everything except power and hierarchy. A man who thought war was a business, who fought a man who thought it was art. Difficult to know which is the more morally despicable.

On Wellington's plinth you can look into the first-floor windows of the house a grateful nation bequeathed to him – No.1 London. Then they came back and broke every pane on Waterloo Day when he was our most loathed prime minister ever. Behind the house is the huge Waterloo memorial. It is everything that Jagger's gunners aren't. A great classically idealized portrait of Achilles, except for a fig leaf that was added

later after horrified nannies pushing prams in the park com-
plained that the minds of their charges were being corrupted.
Ironically, Achilles is made out of melted-down cannons. The
reality of war transformed into the myth of glory.

The other memorial on Hyde Park Corner is the one to the
Machine-Gun Regiment. It was made by Derwent Wood, the
man who – with Lutyens – originally applied to do the gunners.

The machine-gun and the howitzer were the grim reapers of
the Great War, both modern industrial things that scythed away
the last vestiges of the nineteenth century. But Wood has gone
back to the old muscular Christian classical model for his statue,
and it's one of the very few real duds among English war
memorials – a statue of naked David leaning on Goliath's sword.
You can see what he was getting at, the symbol of the little boy
killing the mighty Goliath with a projectile.

On one side of the plinth are the Regiment's awful casualty
figures; it was short-lived as a regiment. On the other face is the
bluntly appropriate quote from the bible: 'Paul has slain his
thousands and David his tens of thousands.' The statue itself is a
fey nod to Donatello but without the kinky greaves and hat. The
pert boarding-school bum moons enticingly out over the traffic
as it shuffles towards Piccadilly. It's a camply workmanlike
vision of High Church art, a parable in bronze, and it couldn't be
more unlike the effect or the experience of machine-guns.
Almost as an after thought, a pair of Lewis guns sit either side of
the plinth with wreaths draped over their barrels. They've been
deliberately made to look decorative, like bookends, or table-
lighters. They could have been putti, or lions, or urns.

Hyde Park Corner is a directory of English metaphor and
symbolism. The highest accolade for these memorials to the
Great War was that at the end of the Second World War, right
across the country, new names and dates were simply appended
to the existing stone. Nobody felt hard done by or second-best;

they were a simple solemn witness and had lost none of their power. The English put so much time and effort into getting them right because they felt they owed it to the dead and the bereaved; but, more than any other nation, they also wanted to commemorate and acknowledge their fallen.

Uniquely, the English think of war as being something they are good at. The English are a martial nation. The Scots and Irish might like to raise the point of order, that what the English are good at is getting Celts to fight their wars for them – at Waterloo only one in 25 soldiers on the battlefield was an Englishman. All nations tell lies about their military prowess, but the English have had an unfeasibly long run of victories. Just sitting here, I can't think of a war they've lost since the American War of Independence – as long as you don't count the Cod War with Iceland, or Suez.

Americans like to think that they won the war of 1812, but that's only because their teaching of history is even more partisan than North Korea's. Few Englishmen know about the war of 1812, for good reason – it's possibly the most ridiculous international war ever fought, and that includes the War of Jenkins' Ear. It was ostensibly about British war ships boarding American merchant ships to pressgang their sailors. Actually, it was about the expansion of the United States into Canada. The English marched down the Eastern Seaboard and burnt the White House. The two sides realized it was an unbearably expensive and pointless conflict, and signed the Treaty of Paris as a technical draw. The real winner of the war of 1812 was Canada, which emerged with a much stronger sense of its own destiny, Canadians having fought effectively to defend their right to self-determination; and it fixed a border that Americans always tell you is the longest undefended border in the world, though I've yet to hear a Canadian mention it.

A military cynic might say that the English have always been very careful *who* they chose to fight – the Army may punch above its weight, but it's generally thumping people well below it. Colonial wars were unpleasant, small massacres and police actions where European technology was ruthlessly used against sticks and stones. Without doubt the bravest people at Rorke's Drift were the Zulus; the Europeans were firing breech-loading rifles from behind breastworks, against people with only a knife on a stick and a leather coffee table. English governments have spent a great deal of time and trouble avoiding fighting punitive or experimental wars for the very sound reason that they're incredibly expensive. What you gain is never worth what you risk losing. The English will pay people off, retreat and go the long way round rather than fight. The Zulu war was a terrible mistake made by a devious twit who was disobeying orders. Even by English and colonial standards, Lord Chelmsford was a fantastically inept, stupid and stubborn man. The Empire was overseen by a string of governments desperate to restrain excitable, vainglorious and bored officers and curb avaricious local politicians.

The belief that they were good at war was useful for the English. They rode their self-made reputation – a threat is always cheaper than a regiment – but it came with an equally copper-bottomed reputation for fair play and a decent even-handed justice and incorruptibility.

It was Churchill who remade the fable of martial England into a cod-scientific eugenics promoting the fortuitous coming-together of the most aggressive and glorious peoples, as if its nation-building were divine dog-breeding. The Celts fought the Saxons, who fought the Normans, then all together they produced a mongrel champ, with a unique mixture of ferocity, skill and discipline, whose fist was ever-ready for the knock-down blow. This self-belief in the peculiar breeding for war was far older than Churchill's war. The Georgians and Victorians believed in their unbeatable regiments with a mathematically precipitous hubris: one highlander would be worth ten dagoes, four wops, fifteen chinks, or twelve fuzzy-wuzzies.

The nation of shopkeepers took a double book-keeping pride in their military. Churchill consciously echoes Shakespeare, who himself must have been touching on some truism for his audience. A belief in the macho good nature of a nation is a central plank of everyone's patriotism, but the English get something different out of blood, death and fear. They don't have the collective sense of glory that the French aspire to. The huge parades of tanks and rockets and soldiers and nurses and boy scouts that newer, more insecure countries indulge in to commemorate the size of their constitutions and testicles is foreign to the English.

The only parades they have are of the toy-soldier sort in dressing-up-box uniforms. They are conspicuously and purposely un-aggressive. The Brigade of Guards reminds the English not of wars but of sitting-room carpets and toy forts and nanny; a cosy homeliness rather than bodies in a field. The bearskins and red tunics are subsidized by the Tourist Board – peevishly, the Army insists that they carry the latest rifle, which makes them look oddly kitsch in the manner of novelty telephones or jokey coffee mugs. They're a practical utensil gussied up to be tweely ornamental.

The English are embarrassed by overt displays of military boasting, the commemorative societies like the Sealed Knot that re-enact battles and fuss over pikes and flints and the correct way to handle a halberd; and what are the authentic songs to sing in the beer tent? 'Ah sweetly needy collection of outward-bound train-spotters in unfanciable dress.'

There is no hatred or vainglorious bellicosity in this role-playing, it's all very limp-wristed. England is one of the only countries in the world where you'll see people dressed up as soldiers from 1640, but not from the present. Military personnel aren't allowed to wear their uniforms in public in peace-time.

Kipling famously wrote about the English expecting miracles from Tommy Atkins when the drum beats rolled, but wanting nothing to do with him when it was all over:

Oh, it's Tommy this, an' Tommy that, an' 'Tommy go away';
But it's 'Thank you, Mister Atkins,' when the band begins to
   play.

This may infuriate majors and snug-bar sentimentalists, but it's actually a surprisingly rational and far-sighted view for a nation. The purpose of an army must surely be to put itself out of business.

England has never died by the sword because it has never lived by the sword. It's been a ghastly bully and thrown its weight around and been sadistic and racist and unfair, but English governments, even during the centuries of its greatest power, have always done their utmost to avoid actually having to fight anyone. The downside of losing was far greater for the English than for any of their potential opponents. The real power of any military force, the English learned very early on, is at its most effective when you don't use it. The most successful example of this is the Royal Navy. Napoleon said that his war with the English was an elephant against a whale – England's greatest asset was afloat, Napoleon's was on land. And in the end, it was the Navy that first contained and then beat Napoleon, and HMS *Bellerophon*, which fought at Trafalgar, which then carried the emperor post-Waterloo to St Helena.

It was the successful blockade of France that precipitated the invention of canned food. The French Navy found it increasingly difficult to find ports where they could re-victual. Even by the unspeakable standards of nineteenth-century navies, a ship of the line got through a lot of food, so they needed a way of preserving it.

Ships often used turtles, which could be stacked alive like

cornflake boxes for up to six months. A French chemist discovered that if you heated pork and beans to 240–265°F in a sealed container they stayed anaerobically edible indefinitely; unfortunately all the pots he used exploded under the pressure. France only manufactured one thing that was strong enough and ubiquitous enough and cheap enough to feed the Navy – champagne bottles. With their thick glass and dimpled bottoms and wired corks, they were designed to resist the pressure of fermentation. So one of the great social boons and culinary disasters of life was invented by the French. They don't like it when you remind them they're responsible for baked beans and, alas, it didn't make their Navy any more effective.

The English Navy didn't have to fight a major engagement between Trafalgar and Jutland, which was an inconclusive battle. The English lost the most ships, but the Germans lost the most nerve, withdrew and never left port again. They failed to break the blockade, and this would eventually starve German civilians into demanding a peace.

The English Navy, since its inception by Alfred, has arguably been the most successful and efficient martial construct ever made. It went on longer than the Roman legions, achieved more than Alexander's hoplites, Tamerlane and the Khans' cavalry, and it did so almost entirely by threats and blockades, and being too expensive to risk using.

Military ability is a load-bearing beam in the English construction of themselves. The dusty names on the colours are the source of collective pride, even if hardly anyone can place them on a map. But there is something else in the English relationship with war, something more equivocal and something I've never seen anywhere else. The Royal Welch Fusiliers at one time had an officers' mess that included Ben Nicholson, Robert Graves, Siegfried Sassoon and David Jones. Now that's quite something. There have been very few university common-rooms that could boast that much artistic and literary talent. It's a lot more of something than the eleven VCs awarded to the Warwickshire regiment that became the Welsh Borderers at Rorke's Drift. But in the fusiliers' mess there was a hint of the contradiction about the English and war.

The English are essentially an angry people, and that anger has driven them to achievement and greatness in a bewildering pantheon of disciplines. At the core of that anger is the knowledge that they could go absolutely berserk with an axe if they didn't bind themselves with all sorts of restraints, of manners, embarrassment and awkwardness and garden sheds. The military and war calls for people to go mad with axes. It's a particularly risky business for the English as, once they start, they might never finish. It could go on until they've chopped up everything, destroyed themselves and the world, until they are nothing but frothing and gibbering monsters sated on blood-lust. But if you look at their war memorials, the soldier reading the letter in Paddington Station, the calm artillery men, there is a serenity, a quiet reflection about the English at war.

They have a subtle and complex relationship with justified violence. There is a dichotomy at the heart of their pride at being good at it; it lives with the *shame* of being good at it. And a fear – not of death or failure – but that this might be who they really are, that opening yourself to violence and righteous anger, throwing off the restraints of the world, might be to throw away everything except for the fury. And they might never be able to get it back again. It's like being a superhero in reverse. The real strength is not in exercising your shattering power, but in keeping your underpants on inside your trousers.

The reason the English disband their forces with reckless haste after wars, why they won't allow their soldiers to walk around in uniform, why there is so little state-sponsored glorification of battle, is because they know where it leads. Far better to do the business as brutally and efficiently as possible and then get back to whatever you were doing before, as fast as is decent. The

American Apache – what's left of them – sit apart. They don't mix with other Indians or with white men, and when they meet others they talk with their heads averted, they won't look anyone directly in the eye. They're not being rude, it's just too dangerous, too provocative to catch a glance. It might unlock something so destructive that it couldn't survive. There is a little of that in the English.

All that art and poetry in the Welch Fusiliers' mess didn't nurture pacifism or intellectually justified cowardice or diplomacy; it was more complicated than that, more English. The Fusiliers' website today doesn't mention the poets or artists at all. There is a page on Sassoon, but it's devoted to the semi-automatic pistol that he bought from the Army & Navy Stores and which the regimental museum now owns. Not mentioning a handful of the greatest war poets – ever – is so farcically English. You'd think young men interested in a military life might read *Goodbye to All That*, or *Memoirs of an Infantry Officer*, or *In Parenthesis*.

It's become a truism of the Great War that the men who fought it came home and never spoke of it. There's a song about them not talking about it – 'We'll never tell them . . .' They wrote reams of letters, volumes of memoirs, but they said very little. On paper it's the most profound and elegant outpouring of literature to spring from a single subject in the English language. Their silence has become a mark of collective English pride; this generation of witnesses to the abiding horror of the century kept it bottled up, muttering it only to each other. They held the horrors and the sadness and the loneliness to their chest. That is such an aridly English virtue: the telling silence, the deafening unsaid.

My grandfather, who fought all through the war and was wounded and lost his best friend beside him, was in the Tank Regiment. He never mentioned the war, though we all knew it was always there, hidden in the rose-beds, hanging in his wardrobe with his regimental tie, red, brown and green – through the mud and the blood to the green fields beyond. Even as a small boy I knew all about Granddad and the war, and knew not to mention it. On Sundays he'd stand at the sideboard and sharpen the carving knife and slice the beef, and after that he'd fall asleep in his armchair, and at four o'clock he'd wake up and peel an orange with a silver knife, and put brass-band music on the gramophone. And I'd march up and down, carrying his walking-stick like a rifle, and he'd teach me the drill. Now that seems poignant to me. He died when I was nine and that's my strongest memory of him. That, and when he carved the beef. He would dip a square of bread in the warm blood, sprinkle it with salt and give it just to me. He was a man who would have been deaf to the symbolism that pricked my thumbs, he didn't deal in similes or metaphors, he had a head full of the real thing.

The English find a release, a simplicity and a terrible familiar beauty in war. It is also not by chance that their medals and awards for doing it well are so paltry and dull, like swimming medals or house prizes. Extremes of anything are very un-English, displays of extravagant bravery are showy and slightly embarrassing; useful, no doubt, but not to be encouraged. Men who've been moved to fits of valour should atone for them with blushing apologies. 'It was nothing. Don't know what got into me.'

Now, ninety years after the first war and sixty years after the second, there has been another slew of war memorials erected by people who don't want to forget – for very different reasons – who need to memorialize in a contemporary and nostalgic way. There's a bland gate erected to the dead of the Empire and the Commonwealth that's a meek imitation of Lutyens. It patronizes countries that have long since shrugged off the nannying of colonialism and are quite capable of remembering their own dead. There is an Australian memorial next door to the gunners, a small copy of the Vietnam memorial in Washington, which in itself was a homage to the memorial at Thiepval, but instead of the names of the glorious dead it has the names of the dull towns and villages that the glorious dead came from before they were glorious.

There is a new memorial to women who served in the Second World War – it's a cube with hats and coats hanging off it. Apparently symbolizing jobs done by women, but with its leaden literalism it misses the point of memorials and just reminds you of housework and faceless drudgery. Most speechlessly, jaw-droppingly awful of all, there is the memorial for animals who died in all conflicts. A huge installation in the central reservation of Park Lane, it's a great curved wall through which bronze animals pass – a camel, a dog, a horse, a pigeon. As an object it is utterly hideous, a limp and thudding rendition of the obvious and the grimly sentimental. It is the final anthropomorphism, the Disneyfication of war. It was relentlessly lobbied for by big-hearted committees of people, and I suppose in the end nobody could come up with a good enough reason not to let them get on with it, or perhaps not a reason as good as the most obvious one, that not all suffering is relatively equivalent, that only humans fight wars, win them, lose them and mourn the loss of those who die in them. If you memorialize the horse that pulled the limbers and the pigeons that carried the messages, how in all conscience can you not remember the cattle that made the bully-beef and the chickens that made the soup? Why don't you put up a statue to Isaac Rosenberg's cosmopolitan rat?

It's not that this thing insults the dead or sullies their memory – they are safe from that. You can't touch the dead, only offend the living, and the tears and loss that are spent on war memorials grow less each year, and that's a good thing. In a short time the Great War will cease to be held in the cradle of living memory, and will slip from the modern age and will become like past wars, a thing of interest, of minute textual argument and intellectual pleasure for specialists. And that's no bad thing either. Maybe the one thing better than a marvellous war memorial is a really dreadful one. Whilst the gunners and the Cenotaph say something profound about the English, so too does the wall for dead dogs.

5

Class

The quartet of my great-grandfathers were, as far as fallible memory tells, an unskilled mill-worker, a farmer, a sailor and a cooper. Further back than that they seem to have been a hazy collection of agricultural labourers, cowboys in Colorado and coolies in Bengal. We don't go in for ancestor worship in our house for obvious reasons. There are no escutcheons or titles, no etchings of defunct statues, no military honours, inventions or discoveries. The Gills and the distaff Gilans, the Tailors and the Baileys all appear to have been hard-working souls whose aspirations stretched no further than their own front doors.

They were, with the exception of some nineteenth-century mill-owners, resolutely manual working class. At the turn of the twentieth century they set out on the trajectory that marks the thrust and purpose of the modern age. My paternal grandfather returned from the Great War and married the girl he found understudying his clerking job in the bank. She was the daughter of the mill-owners who were gently descending the class ladder, he was the son of a mill-worker who bettered himself and ended up as a bank manager in Cheltenham. They had a single son.

On the other side, my grandfather fought in the French Army – by his own account modestly refusing to become an officer – and came to Edinburgh to study engineering until his money ran out and he became a working-man's dentist. He married a local woman who had great dreams of bettering herself, but had left it rather too late, and this little dark Frenchman was her best last hope. They had a happy marriage, even though he turned out years later not to have been exactly what he had allowed people to imagine. Actually, he was an Indian. They had a single daughter. My father left the RAF after the Second World War and was the first member of his family ever to go to University. He studied philosophy and psychology at Edinburgh, where he met the dentist's daughter, who was an actress. They married. He worked as a sub-editor on the *Scotsman* and she bore their first child, who turned out to be me. He got a job with the BBC and they moved to London.

I pass all this on because I've always thought that we are a typical example of the journey into the middle class that millions and millions of families made in the three generations of the twentieth century. From farm labourer through industrial worker to clerk to bank manager and dentist, to actress and TV producer and finally to me, a journalist, the quintessential middle-class occupation. Journalists are naturally loathed and despised by the middle classes, whilst at the same time they're all jolly happy and supportive if their children want to have a go after leaving what we called Varsity, and they now call Uni. Odd how the truncation simply skips a syllable.

No foreigner could ever write a book about the English without at least one chapter on the class system, or perhaps larding every chapter with the class system, seeing everything from food to clothes to politics through the prism of class. Books, papers, magazines and all the rest of the media are where the class system now lives.

I started as a journalist on *Tatler* – England's oldest and most forthrightly snobbish magazine. We wrote eternally and exhaustively about class, spreading the thin joke of U and non-U, ever more gossamer-thinly. We would sit in the office and ask in a bored sort of way whether cufflinks with semi-precious stones worn in the daytime were common or bohemian, or what sort of cake/envelope/haircut was smart this week. There was nothing so innocuous that it couldn't be passed through the napkin ring (v. common) of class. We knew that our readership were mostly girls who washed other girls' hair for a living. We also knew they read it for the pleasure of puffing out their cheeks, rolling their eyes and exclaiming: 'Have you ever heard anything so stupid as this.' Maybe there were a few hundred deeply insecure women who hung on to our every word as social gospel, but I expect they can't have lasted long in the temporal world.

I feel no guilt about admitting that we made the whole thing up. It was a game with moves as rigorous and convoluted as mah-jong, but with slightly less point. It was like playing with a model railway. The world we invented all looked fascinatingly life-like if you got down on your hands and knees and screwed your eyes up. The point about class is that it is a conceit, a plot device. Class in England is a cultural form, like farce or limericks. It has a set of rules that everyone in the country understands; they just don't apply to anyone's real life today and haven't for the last generation. Any argument that depends on class for its structure will quickly dissolve into a Jesuitical dissection of definitions of terms. What do you mean by working class, upper class, the sub-divisions of middle class?

I once interviewed Tony Benn and, as many of his marvellously humane and winningly formless pronouncements involved nods to, or active participation in, a working class, I asked him for his definition. Was I, for instance, a member? The great thing about talking to him was that no question was remotely original or came to him for the first time. He was like a marvellously practised haberdasher; he simply reached up for the box with miscellaneous definitions and answers, and out came the right one. Yes, of course I was working-class – I was paid a wage, I worked for an international conglomerate; being freelance was no freedom, simply less protection. Fortunately, the definition of the working class was broadly anyone who could be sacked. Well, that's pretty much everyone, including the monarch.

'Many captains of industry didn't realize they were members of the working class until they were told to leave the building without clearing their desks,' he said with relish. The class system, and the beauty and romantic destiny of the workers, was so much part of his personal mythology that, rather than saying the industrial hand that had made the nineteenth-century paradigm was obsolete, in classic Old Labour style, he just co-opted more workers to fill the empty pews. So in the end, his church was full of non-believers, but at least it was full.

The class system in any meaningful, usable, worthwhile, mutually agreed form doesn't exist in England. I'm going to have to say that again, just so there's no doubt. There is no class system. It's an ex-class system. It's still used of course, its coffin is still dragged out. People will still pepper their speech, or more likely their writing, with references to the working class or the aristocracy or the bourgeoisie, although 'bourgeoisie' is a bit intellectually poly-radical now. The labels are applied more to add colour than weight. When Mrs Thatcher said there was no such thing as society, she infuriated many acolytes of class to the point of rolling effervescence. Far worse than sinking the *Belgrano*, or filling in the mines, it was because that seemed to cut the binding of the nation. If we weren't a society, then what were we? And the good of society is surely above and beyond politics. 'No such thing as society' was like saying there was no such thing as us. 'No such thing as society' was a round robin, dear John letter saying we'd been dumped.

Actually, snobbishly, I like to think that Mrs Thatcher meant society in the *Tatler* sense. In the Nancy Mitford sense. An end to society as a closed shop with pearls, an end to the freemasonry of U and non-U and the snobbish gang acronyms: plu (people like us), hklp (holds knife like pen), fhb (family holdback), gib (good in bed), gibnfs (good in bed not fit for society). If that's the society that doesn't exist any more then I'm all for it, having spent so many years inventing it.

The great achievement of the twentieth century was the movement of the working class into the middle, which also reached out and consumed the upper. The triumph of the centre has always been the point and the goal, and pretending it isn't is wilful blindness. The rise and complete victory of the middle class is a marvellous achievement. A great victory. But naturally it's seen as a vile mediocrity, not least by itself. The victorious middle class bullies itself for being itself. The long and tortured stream of masochism that is the abiding, shameful feature of England and the English turns into drawing-room self-ridicule. The yearning for a class system is yet another aspect of the narcissism of nostalgia. The class system seems so cosy in retrospect; everyone knew their place, and the objectives of the workers were so noble and the life of the aristocracy so elegant.

Class is used by the English as a shorthand for character; they love plays and black-and-white films where class is an effortless code, an engine of narrative. So much of English culture, design and history seems to be built on the three pillars of class that to simply let it go and admit that it's done its job, that the aristocracy who husbanded rural England and the workers who built industrial England have died off and left us with middle-class England, is too sad. The loss of the class system as a meaningful or manipulable social tool is like the loss of empire. It's gone. But the English can still feel it, a phantom ache of longing.

Class isn't just a reminder of those better times, class was the very structure of life. It was the great excuse – every nation needs a great excuse, and class belonged to the English. If you didn't get on, if the marriage failed or the kids turned out bad, it could all be put down to class. Yours or someone else's. It was a wonderful, subtle and direct, ever warm and welcoming excuse for righteous anger. The English could wallow in class, for a couple of minutes in a shop, or for a few hours in the pub, or even devoting a whole lifetime to the ire of the downtrodden, the put-upon and the misunderstood. Class had the assumption and the status of English DNA, a Darwinian certainty, the immovable three legs of a stool. A chair with four legs rocks on uneven ground, but a stool always stands solid, is sure-footed. So the three legs of the class system seemed to keep England stable.

The class system was worn away by mass culture, universal health, better housing, cheap travel, mass employment, big cities, pop music, divorce, more sex, more drugs, more people and more immigration, but mostly it was elbowed because it was too fucking incorrigibly stupid. Stupid and slow. Stupid, inept and clunky. Stupid and awkward and ugly and just plain embarrassing. The class system was a bad, rude, unpleasant thing, and getting nostalgic about class is like missing your own shit. People who go on about it are sniffing toilet paper.

But of course, class didn't just vanish. Just as every drop of water that was here at the creation is still here in some form or other, so every bad idea an Englishman ever came up with is still out there somewhere. Class got minced and remade into little disposable, bite-sized sneers of throwaway types: yuppies and chavs, Essex girls and wiggers, trustafarians, Sloane rangers, Mondeo man. Class became the effluent of the focus group and the marketing consultant. A construct of Sunday supplements, lads' mags and TV psephologists. No longer the legs of society, it became a transient selection on a menu of fashionable snobbery. The name-calling and pigeon-holing comes and goes. One moment the world seems to be full of dinkies, the next it's overrun with hoodies. And this makes England seem an unexpectedly exciting place of competing and confederating tribes. IKEA meets the Lord of the Rings. None of the definitions are important or powerful enough to be a proper hindrance to anyone, all of them add a little something to England's threadbare tapestry. It's an adolescent view of society and culture, seen as an extension of mods and rockers, punks and skinheads, Goths, nerds and jocks – but with one difference. Kids choose a gang to join and then they grow out of it. The shorthand definitions of contemporary England, of the advertising gurus and style editors are not those of the members of the clubs. No one planned on being a yuppy or works at being a chav. All these snide little definitions of new society are imposed from outside. It's name-calling, bullying.

When the old three-tier class system went, it took the nasty but satisfying drawing-room vice of snobbery with it. Overt displays of old class one-upmanship now look as smart as a wet patch on the front of your trousers. The growth of the middle class is often said to be what developing Third World countries need to lift them out of poverty and into probity. It rather begs the chicken to provide the egg. Is the middle class a symptom or a catalyst? Do you get it when things are on the up or will they not elevate until you make one? What is obviously true is that without a middle class, you get 21st-century problems in a medieval society.

The least important thing about a middle class is its ability to make money. Its desire for stability and growth and culture are what really changes societies. Liberalism, the particularly self-flagellating invention of the bourgeoisie, is the politics of permanent concern; the defining liberal characteristic is being able to see both sides of every argument, for which it is roundly mocked by those who can only see the end of their noses. And as it was in the aristocrats' nature to slowly die out through breeding, and the working class's destiny to build itself obsolete, so it is the middle class's desire to disband as soon as possible.

The definition of middle class has become so blandly all-encompassing that it is almost meaningless. My grandfather, my father and I have marked between us, along with millions of others, the flowering of the middle class like one of those exotic plants in Kew that grow with an ugly determination for a hundred years before blooming with a mighty effort and an awful stink, and with the effort passing away.

My children, if they choose to live in England, may well be the first generation that grows up in a society without a hierarchical class system. They will be able to be in more than one class at a time, be one thing at home, another at work, another at night and another on holiday. They'll be able to graze from gang to gang. But a country without a class system is not a classless country. This Utopian happy-ending society is not a destination, it's an evolution, and something else will grow in its place. And being England and the English, whatever it is they construct between them, you can be sure that it'll be unpleasant, unfair, cruel and above all smug.

I once met a lovely gynaecologist and obstetrician – how often do you get to say that? She was from South Carolina and was delivering the Navajo in Colorado. 'Good at having babies, the Navajo,' she said. 'They've got good pelvises and well-shaped heads. I was a doctor in England, you know, for a year in Somerset.' We were sitting on top of 700 foot of rock looking out over the gullies and shimmering wind and water-carved red cliffs of the desert. It was difficult to conjure up Somerset. After a pause, she said: 'You people, you people. I was a registrar in a big hospital. When a new patient was admitted I was told to fill in their class at the top of the form. "What?" I said. "Their class", I was told. It wasn't upper, middle or lower, it was a, b, c and d, but it's the same thing. Upstairs downstairs. "Why?" I said. "Well it helps us with the diagnosis and treatment," they said. "Why don't we just examine them?" I asked, and they smiled like you're smiling. "Anyway," I said, "how am I supposed to know what their class is? Do I ask them? Do you have certificates or badges or tattoos?" And they coughed and shuffled and said that I could get an idea from an accent. And I said, "I couldn't tell the difference between Australian and Glasgow." Anyway, one day I was on the ward with a consultant and he said, "That lady over there, did you notice her luggage?" "What, her overnight bag?" "Yes, very nice, very good luggage," he said, as if he were teaching me some subtle symptom, a diagnostic indicator. He went round the hospital surreptitiously eyeing up luggage. You people. You treat people like suitcases. We were treating fucking suitcases.'

6

Humour

England and the English claim two muses as their own. The first is history and the second is humour. The English also know that they have more jokes worth telling than anyone else. A sense of humour is as necessary to being English as a sense of the past. To accuse an Englishman of lacking or losing his sense of humour is to question the very id of his being. To banish him from his tribal Blightiness. The ability to give and take a joke is almost a definition of being English, and the inability is often used as the demarcation line between belonging and being other – a foreigner.

So I went in search of funny old England. Every city in the country has a gigglish mad-cap comedy venue, an upstairs room where people will try to make you laugh for a fiver. *Time Out*, London's entertainment listings magazine, has six pages devoted to comedy for a week. On a Wednesday you can choose from twenty-one separate performances, most of them with multiple comics; that's a lot of punch lines fed into the English gut of jollity.

I stuck in a pin and turned up at the Intrepid Fox, where I was promised a comedy cabaret. 'Joe Romero hosts his small and friendly club where anything goes, as established and newer acts try out new material and characters. Open spots available on the night. £5, or £4 if you bring a copy of this magazine.'

Like most people who live within walking distance, I rarely go to Soho at night. It's a suburb in the heart of London. The province of out-of-townies, provincial office parties, last-train youths, questing tourists and northern truants. Soho's pleasures are no longer aimed at me or most Londoners. I used to come here a lot. Twice in my life I've worked in Soho, and I was at art school on its northern fringes. In many ways, it's the most old-fashioned part of the city. Its erotica still has a fifties seediness, an aura of luncheon vouchers, Ascot immersion heaters, garter belts and compacts, novelty ashtrays, chiffon scarves with poodles and Eiffel Towers draped over bedside lamps.

A slight and scrawny prostitute in tracksuit bottoms and comfy slippers and scraped back death-coloured hair shimmied up to me at the corner of Berwick Street, and asked if I'd like to spend some time with her. 'Just come up and have a look – no commitment,' she said chummily. I wondered if she wanted me to inspect the room or her intimate work equipment. Being English, I expect it will have been the furniture. 'You have made it nice up here – I like the little rug, and you can't beat candlewick. Yes, this will do me fine for ten minutes' how's your father. Ooh thank you, I'd love one, two lumps and just as it comes.'

The old post-war denizens and wardens of Soho, those yellowing, tweedy, piss-stained literary sclerotics who rolled around like random pinballs getting ejected from one sagging pub after another, were, for a brief time, my low-life heroes. They've all gone now, all those angry young men who grew to be irrationally irritated old women, with a copy of yesterday's *Times* folded three ways in their jacket pocket so that the crossword could be eked out over a pint filled up with periodic halves. They had all been drunk with Dylan and been hit by Behan, and they all owed each other money; their lives a careful seesaw of cheques and balances. It was the Coach, then the French and an afternoon in the disgusting Petri dish of the Colony Club where you might see Francis or Lucian, but you never did.

It wasn't that they were all drunk so much as that they had all been drunk for so long. What I remember most about Soho in the seventies was the incontinence. Soggy bar stools and abandoned knickers. The ding-dong (double Bells) and Navy Cut would gather them into friendless ashes, dumped back in the northern grit from which years before they'd emerged, charging, roaring like spring bullocks, hearts of brass, mouths full of brown bitter and malt vinegar, molten talent and anvil ambition, all spent an epigram and an adjective at a time in book reviewing and pamphlets for the GPO and in the pub. Or they'd top themselves in rent-controlled rooms above delicatessens surrounded by tear-stained first editions. And then there'd be a pissy, brown-toothed wake with incoherent toasts of pastis down the French, and it would end in a fight as a pair of skid-stained, stinky, baby-haired, nicotine-taloned men of letters would come to air-swinging fisticuffs about who fucked some long dead, deranged French poet first.

They always said that old literary Soho should be a school or a movement. It should have been recognized like po-faced, snotty Bloomsbury the other side of Oxford Street, but it never really caught on, principally because none of the old gits managed to write the book.

I mention all that because I want to point out that Soho isn't an intrinsically funny place. It's not the seaside, it's not a laugh a minute. Actually, it's deeply sad. A mile of thwarted, exploited, avaricious and cruel little backrooms made nastier by the daytime presence of the film, TV and advertising industries and their concomitant hangers-on and familiars. That's not to say it hasn't got excitement, entertainment and some dingy charm. But it's just not funny. It's an unkind place, and the last thing I remember about the old Soho literary lot was their vicious, sparkling cruelty to each other. The remorseless, lacerating, deconstruction of all that they loved, their attachments and hopes. There was no let-up, no quarter. You were supposed to grin and bear the mockery, the bitchery and the relentless undermining. Because this was England and you had to take a joke.

I hadn't been to the Intrepid Fox for thirty years. I particularly remember the last time, when I was a shop assistant in an artists' materials shop in Broadwick Street. We used to get a lot of advertising men in, and one of them offered me a job. It was after lunch. 'You're too smart to work here,' he said. 'You'd be brilliant in advertising. Meet me in the Intrepid Fox.' He looked embarrassed when I turned up, bought me a drink and apologized that he had to dash. I drank my beer and left. The Fox was then a faux Edwardian boozer full of creatives talking too loudly.

Walking in three decades later I found that it had all been painted black. Its walls were covered in posters of palely-peeved pop singers, striking poses of colonic blockage. Behind the bar there was a small ossuary of plastic sculls and around the dado rail a tableau of a graveyard, with polystyrene tomb stones and dead plants. Over all crashed and thudded the hectic shriek of thrash metal kept at the level of a force nine gale.

The Fox had morphed into a coven for Goths. The bar staff were a pair of skeletal men who had levered themselves into excruciating denim, and bore the sort of tattoos that reduce your career options to roadying in Finland or being a barman in a Goth pub. One had a tiny black t-shirt that said 'It's rock and fucking roll' like a health warning. The customers were mostly Gothic, ranging from radical, multi-pierced zombies to not so much 'the un-dead' as just 'the feeling a little under the weather', wearing Army surplus grey coats and Himalayan acne; there were one or two Brides of Dracula and some Beelzebub's bikers' chicks. Newly damned souls would walk in and make the sign of the antichrist at the barman, who cheerily signalled back the evil eye and pulled a pint of the usual. They would then retreat to the wall and bang their heads ruminatively.

Just visible through the cobwebbed cemetery was the Regency

bust, originally by Nollekens, of the intrepid Charles James Fox himself, the Bacchanalian gambler, seducer, supporter of revolutions, radical reformer, habitual opposer, bankrupt refuser of bribes and most intemperate, insulting, argumentative and greatest orator of his age. Fox is the absentee father of the Liberal Party. He was a politician who spent all but a few brief moments of his lengthy career on the Opposition benches, but still managed to be more of an influence on the nation than most of those in Government. Finally, days before he died, he signed the Bill to abolish slavery and had his name scrubbed from the list of privy councillors for having offered the toast 'to our monarch, the people'. I imagine Fox would have quite liked having the Goths in his pub. He was certainly hairy enough and smelly enough.

Fox is a very good example of an angry Englishman. A man who managed to remain furious all his political life. Anger and conflict didn't burn themselves out or become exhausted, they simply moved on to find more fuel, to suck in more oxygen for more heat. He was a one-man firestorm, who couldn't help singeing everyone around him. He is like so many English heroes. A man who is admirable and amusing from a posthumous distance, but must have been utterly impossible to be close to. Fox is that most venerated, Anglo-Saxon archetype – the bully. And bullying is mostly what the English sense of humour is for.

I ordered my drink at the bar and asked the barman where the Comedy Store was, and I said it twice more to get over the barbed wire of metal music. He looked quizzical and called over another flying-haired nerdy hell-fiend with Tolkienesque articulated knuckle-rings. 'Do we have a Comedy Store?' 'Yes,' said the dragon-fist with a strong German accent, 'but it doesn't start for about an hour. You go out there, past the toilets and up the stairs.'

There is a book to be written about the rooms above pubs –

they are the moots, the workshops, the laboratories and rehearsal rooms, the alternative surgeries and secret conclaves of the English. Into everybody's life at some point there will be a trip to a room above a pub. Here meet the variegated, spectacled and cardiganed inventory of appreciation societies, from fancy canaries to polkas and Goon Show re-enactors. Above pubs collect and conjugate miserly numismatists (coins); punctual horologists (clocks); bibulous tegestologists (beer mats); lonely cartophilists come to meet like-minded phillumenists – non-smokers preferred – (cigarette cards and matchboxes). Thick-skinned coleopterists (beetles); loveable arctophilists (teddy bears), the secret migrant oologists (birds' eggs) and copoclephilists, not to be confused with coprophiles (respectively key rings and shit).

Here people come for self-help, to take twelve giant steps, empathize, sympathize and criticize. They sidle upstairs to read homemade haikus, learn funnygalore and Viking, weave, fret, knit and stick matchsticks into miniature wonders. There is not a political movement or pressure group that doesn't owe its infancy to a room above the saloon bar. World domination and guinea-pig liberation are planned above pubs. They are the cabinets of curiosities containing the obsessive, compulsive, myopic, untiring, unending weirdness of the English, and people come here to tell jokes.

I sat down and watched the Goths. The background *Sturm und Drang* cancelled itself out and became quite restful, like the hum of a great engine. Of all the youth groups that have rushed in like spring tide and ebbed out like tepid bathwater, the Goths are the most bizarrely inexplicable. It is in the nature and purpose of youth fads to be opaque to those past joining in, but generally you can see that they start either with high aspirations like the hippies who wanted a better world, love and peace; the punks' anarchy and nihilism; or the skinheads who wanted a nation devoted to amphetamines and Third Division football. Or they were excusably hedonistic, like the Teddy Boys, and the New Romantics and Mods were simply expressions of vanity and self-regard. Disco and rave culture was about drugs and dancing, but an entire youth movement based around the works of Mary Shelley is odd.

It's not that Goths appear to be having much fun. The tightness of the clothes, the hugeness of the boots and the spikiness of the piercings exclude dancing with anything more than your hair. Most youth movements are against something grown-up: capitalism, bombs, dinner parties; but Goths seem to be mostly a reaction against the modern novel and cinema vérité. It's the only clan that is actually opposed to enjoyment. Goths are acolytes of suicide, grisly death, mascara and children's fairy stories. Why they should have outlasted all the other more vigorous and attractive movements of the last thirty years is a proper mystery. Maybe all the rest are natural pupations before adulthood, a space for music and pills and the dressing-up box that will sustain you on the long commute of conformity. But being a Goth is a cul-de-sac. A dead end for the un-dead, where the ritual pantomime pessimism and kitsch angst means that you never move on, because there is no point. You just wait for the nerve to light a thousand candles and then hang yourself with a bishop's pyjama cord, or perhaps you just wait for Buffy to come along and stab you through the heart with a broken stick.

Every year Goths congregate in the collar-up fishing town of Whitby on the North Yorkshire coast. The home of Captain Cook – a tough, no-nonsense Yorkshireman who was probably the finest navigator ever. His achievement was only underlined by the chronic bad luck or carelessness of the Dutchman Abel Tasman, who arrived at the southern ocean before him and managed to discover Tasmania – which is Australia's Isle of Wight – and then sailed up the coast of Australia without ever, apparently, noticing it was there.

Whitby used to import great rolling barges of human urine from Newcastle to use in the local alum mines. Since the Stone Age, piss and alum have been used in tanning. Of course, Whitby is also – and more famously – the landing and resting place for Dracula. A boat with a dead crew drifted into the little harbour. On board was a coffin, which the locals interred in the ruined Abbey that stands on the cliff. Except they didn't. Dracula's boat didn't drift here from Carpathia and he's not buried in the Abbey, because it's a fairy story. But still, every Halloween Goths appear in their thousands, all in black and white and all as miserable as local sin. They hang around pubs, drink lager and black, eat cod and chips on the windy wet streets and leave eye-shadow stains on the B&B pillows. Mostly they look bored and fat and cold and misinformed. To make matters ever more humiliating, the locals love them. Tourists are few and far on this stony coast since aeroplanes were invented, so they don't look a gift Goth in the mouth. They print special editions of the local paper with lots of seaside pictures of zombies putting on their best evil-eyes, and they erect banners explaining that Whitby welcomes the Goths and vampires, and the pubs make Ribena cocktails and hang rubber bats in their windows, and you can go and see *Dawn of the Dead* with a bracing early-morning cliff walk on the heritage trail, and the local vicar is available for chats with anyone who feels they'd like to turn stool pigeon against Beelzebub. It's all laughably twee and twinky, and the poor Goths look so doubly bereft confronted with the sniggering banality of their own dark side and the true, ultimate horror of an East Coast seaside resort out of season.

I found the stairs beside the lavatory. At the top was a door. I pushed it open. Inside a little room was a young man standing with his back to me. He was talking to someone I couldn't see, turned and looked surprised. 'Is this the Comedy Club – new and experienced acts trying new material, five quid?' 'Um, no. We're not doing it this week. We're having a séance.' As I walked back down the stairs I heard another voice – perhaps a woman, perhaps a disembodied woman – saying 'You sent them away,' with just a touch of wistful longing. Well, professionals all say comedy is in the timing.

So I walked through Soho to the Crown on Brewer Street, with four televisions showing Chelsea v. Newcastle. The pub was half full of office workers, waylaid on their way to homes too distant and uninviting to arrive at sober. Everyone was looking up, eyes transfixed at a different corner of the room like so many cats watching moths. The saloon-bar upstairs was where they kept the comedy, next to the lavatories again. There was a powerful and effulgent smell of industrial disinfectant. It's a smell that never reassures you about cleanliness; rather, it makes you doubly squeamish of lurking vileness. Soap smells clean, disinfectant smells dirty. Funny that.

It was a very small room, the size of a generous semi's knock-through lounge. There was an unmatched mix of pub chairs set up facing the wall, with a curtain that looked like a prop from a junior school end-of-term play. Cut out letters spelt 'Joe's Comedy Madhouse' (Joe isn't his real name). Madhouse is an unpromising moniker for 'cutting-edge experimental humour'. It's too reminiscent of the fat boy on the school bus who shrieks, 'I'm mad, me, I'll do anything – eat waste paper, pour sugar down me underpants.' I paid my £6 and sat down. After a bit of a wait a bearded young man came on and said, 'Welcome to Joe's Comedy Madhouse, and without more ado here's Sid Zimmerman – your host for the evening. A big hand please.' So we all clapped. When I say all, I mean eight of us, which included the man at the door.

The introductory student beardy did not seem entirely necessary, except that it appears to be a rule of stand-up that everybody has to be introduced by someone else, as in a gentlemen's club. Perhaps he was a comic untouchable who didn't have a name worth introducing himself, or perhaps he was privately introduced downstairs in the pub. The compere was Sid Zimmerman. Sid isn't his real name. Zimmerman is. It used to be Bob Dylan's name too. Maybe it was Sid's branch of the family that made Bob consider changing it to that of a drunk Welsh Soho doggerelist. You could see why.

The first thing you noticed about Sid was that he was supremely ugly. A bony, misshapen face with a fright of hair, that would have been unsalable in the 'Reduced to Clear' bin of a fancy-dress shop the day after Halloween. The individual features of his face might have been stuck on by a six-year-old. Its main point of interest was a mouth like a torn pocket, and a random selection of teeth that were all making a dash for the exit. The next thing you noticed was that he was working himself up into a state of mania, rocking back and forth, skipping and pacing, arms pumping, hands grasping the air as if it were full of invisible breasts. His eyes rotated, his mouth drizzled, he had an unfortunate saliva problem. He produced viscous globules of the stuff, but didn't seem to have anywhere to keep it. Anyway, that was soon forgotten because it was, frankly, the least of his problems, the most pressing of which was that as a comedian he was shit.

Perhaps that's unfair. You can grow tomatoes in shit. Sid only made you want to throw tomatoes. His sorry schtick, for what it's worth, was to be loud, spindly, frenetic and ugly. It's not much of an act. Particularly if you have the timing of an epileptic on roller skates and material that you couldn't even tear up to use as bandages. As a warm-up he was hiccups in a library – and then he picked on me. 'What's your name then? Where you from? What you do? Why you wearing that coat?' I don't much like random audience participation. It's lazy, cruel in the particular and insulting in general. And it has to have a point, an act. Sid had no act. He was just desperately fishing. Actually he wasn't fishing, he was drowning. I was the straw he was grasping at and I did something that was rather unkind.

Rather un-Samaritan. I didn't do anything at all. I didn't say a word. He really needed an answer, needed some communication, a heckle – anything. If you pick on someone in an audience of 500, the other 499 will laugh, partly from relief that it wasn't them. In an audience of eight no one laughs, because they don't want to draw attention to themselves. Sid died – noisily, thrashing hideously. It was the comedy equivalent of Ebola and it was catching.

The next act, who got a big hand, was another unfanciable young man with St Vitus's dance. After every dud set-up, he laughed at himself with a masochistic glee and pointed out that that joke hadn't worked. The rest of us were way ahead of him. Yet another lad followed, sweated and shouted, raised his cardiovascular rate into the high hundreds and expired with the deathly rattle of, 'You've been great, thank you very much . . .' The overwhelming emotion was of acute, possibly harmful embarrassment. In a small room with bright lights, there was nowhere to hide. Embarrassment for the acts, embarrassment for the audience that grew into a sort of self-pitying horror, like a plane crash that never quite hits the ground.

Then it was half time. It had been thirty minutes of Madhouse non-stop comedy, but it seemed longer than *Götterdämmerung*, with fewer laughs. It was three helpings more than enough. I slipped back through the bar and out onto the street. I noticed five of the audience already hailing a cab.

What was so astonishing about this was that it wasn't just done badly, it utterly failed to do it at all. No one would conceivably get up and sing that tone-deafly. No violinist or banjo or tambourine player would advertise this numbness of talent in *Time Out*. Comedy is the only bit of the culture where people who are manifestly and demonstrably bereft of the remotest humour are invited to get up on stage and draw attention to the fact. And on the evidence of this evening you would have a pretty hard time convincing any observant outsider that the English had, not just a lousy sense of humour, but any idea what humour was, and what they refer to as 'having a laugh' and 'taking a joke' is actually something else altogether. And the truth is, I think it probably is.

You have to ask why these young lads were doing it. Standing up in front of a roomful of strangers to make them laugh is the most hyperventilating and stressful event available to a human existence. Doing it because someone's holding your child by the ankles out of a fifteenth-floor window is understandable, doing it for thousands of pounds or because you are one of those rare creatures who are naturally very good at it and can't do anything else is reasonable. Doing it because you have a sort of loony, comic nymphomania ought to be treatable, but doing it because you're young and it's there for not much more than a fiver is imbecilic. Like dressing up as a traffic warden because you want to meet people and make friends. There must be some cultural imperative that makes so many young men get up and try to tell jokes they've made up in the bath. It has something to do with being young, male and ugly.

Humour is England's obsession. Jokes are the English social currency. I doubt that anywhere else takes to catchphrases and television comedy with such gluttonous greed as the English. Tabloid newspapers and lads' magazines are sodden with humour and 'would you believe it' fun. Jokes are e-mailed and texted in a constant ticker-tape stream. English women regularly report, when asked, that a sense of humour is their first requirement in a mate. I doubt if this is true of Indian or Russian women. Making mates and strangers laugh has a higher status in England than it does in almost any other country. In the rest of Europe, being serious is valued more highly than being funny. But in England it's the other way round, and it probably always has been.

Chaucer, the first man in print, was funny – and funny in an identifiably English manner. His language is still wet it's so new.

But he was cracking observational jokes and creating comic characters that were the models for most sitcoms, novels and movies. England produces a lot of comedy, much of it dreadful, repetitive, derivative, pointless, unpleasant and unfunny. It's like birdsong, a conversation that has no real content or meaning. It simply says, 'I'm here, I'm here, I'm still here.'

Jokes are the clannish symbols of belonging, like tribal scarring. Jokes and joke-telling are important to young men because tribal membership is particularly important to young men. Comedy changes with age, but instead of the comedy growing ever more complicated and sophisticated as we grow older, it seems to peak in late adolescence and starts tailing off in middle age, until it's barely Germanic when you retire. So there's a comic heyday of about twenty years, say from fifteen to thirty-five, when the largest slice of professional laughter is aimed at you if you're a man. Look at the audiences for comic shows on television, in theatres, clubs and magazines – almost all young men. And it's young men who want to stand up and tell jokes in rooms above pubs. A sense of humour isn't just a national cultural affinity, it's a large part of the behaviour and motivation of young English blokes. It's having a laugh.

Now I should declare an interest here. I write humour for a living. There's no reason why you should have noticed. I don't do comedy or jokes. I suppose you might call it wit, and the definition of wit is a joke that doesn't make you laugh. The older and more culturally sedate humour gets, the less it makes you laugh until the highly civilized old people will tell you, that of course the thing about T. S. Eliot is that he is so screamingly funny. And they'll say the same about Shakespeare. And I happen to think that a lot of Shakespeare is very funny – or at least it makes me laugh. Not out loud, but in the poker-faced way of middle-aged people in the theatre. I know that Pyramus and Thisbe, the comic turn from *Midsummer's Night Dream*, would die a death at a Comedy Store, or in a room above a pub.

Laughter changes as you get older. It's still about belonging, but it's just to a different club.

So having to sit through somebody's stand-up act after work is, for me, a bit like being a doctor at a dinner party. I don't want to have to listen to other people crack their funny bones after having spent all day tapping my own. But stand-up is to humour what lap-dancing is to dancing. It's laughter without context. It's set-up and punch-line, set-up and punch-line but for no end or purpose other than the pointless laugh. Nothing is gained, nothing changed, nothing made or unmade. It's just having a laugh.

All I want to do during a stand-up act is heckle. I don't want to shout obscenities, or offer wit. I just want to ask what they think they're really doing. What is this all about? Is it about being ugly and unappreciated? Is it a sort of endurance thing, like climbing a cliff? Because it's obviously got nothing do with the audience or the money or the approbation. It's like watching someone have a cathartic moment of self-loathing, auto-humiliation. I never do heckle, of course, but I'm always on the side of the heckler. Whatever they shout, I think: they're actually paramedics trying to talk someone down. Don't do it. Don't tell another joke, life's not that bad. It may seem like it now, but you're young, you don't have to be a stand-up all your life. Really, there's seriousness out there, and it can be yours.

The best heckle I ever heard of was to Kirk Douglas's other son – Zeppo Douglas. He was a drunk and a bit of a druggie and a bit of a lost soul with personal worth issues. So naturally he turned to stand-up. His act was dying in some Hollywood club and in desperation he said: 'You know who I am, I'm Kirk Douglas's son,' and someone in the audience stood up and shouted, 'No, I'm Kirk Douglas's son,' and then another stood up: 'I'm Kirk Douglas's son,' and the whole audience was on its feet. That was a proper moment of Anglo-Saxon humour.

Humour appears to be a nebulous mercurial thing. It comes

out of the air like flu. Sometimes you get it, sometimes you don't. Jokes, situations, lines arrive as if by magic. Who coined the first Englishman, Irishman and Scotsman joke? No one knows. Who started the shaggy dog story or the blonde joke? Who deemed the Irish stupid or the Scots mean?

There is a belief that popular humour is the essence of some collective identity, an alias for who you are, because jokes don't come with authors, they belong to the last mouth they popped out of. So-and-so told me this joke; then it becomes your joke. You pass it on and it's someone else's joke, and by the end of the week it's the nation's joke and is a small patch on the motley of the national costume.

I admit that I hate jokes, I've always loathed them. After the age of thirty anyone who's lived in England has heard every single one. All the new jokes, without exception, are simply variations on some roundelay theme, some threadbare tapped-out seam. You listen to gags move around the world from Paddies to Pakis to Pikies to Poles, from Marilyn Monroe to Posh Spice, those instant e-mail chain jokes that come as the gasp of bad taste in the wake of death and disaster. They are as old as laughing in the face of misery and naughty guilt.

The abiding creation myth of English comedians is that way back in their poor, rough pasts, humour came to them rather like a superhero's unnatural powers as a defence against bullying. Whilst having their heads shoved down the bog for the fifth time, they inadvertently made a noise that sounded like a Jacques Cousteau impression and the big boys let go and said, 'Do that again' and laughed. And that noise, the laughter – not the Jacques Cousteau impression – struck some deep chord and ever after they've wanted to make rough boys laugh, so they hung around Uni bars and the upstairs rooms of pubs. The 'laughter trumps muscle' parable is central to English comedy, the model of the joke as underdog puncturing authority: Jack and the Giant, little Norman Wisdom and Mr Grimsdale. Most

English comic actors and almost all double-acts have a cartoon *faux* idiot David and a pompous know-all Goliath.

In the English comic creation myth humour is the gift of the poor, the working class. The straight man, the butt of the joke, is almost always upper-class, or at least bank-manager class, the one in the bow tie and the suit. The only type of humour that is excused lower classness is satire, and satire is the chamber music of comedy – a joke that many people profess to enjoy, but few actually get. Since Monty Python the preferred birthplace of comics is no longer the back-to-back north, but the lower-middle-class suburbs.

The little man defeating might hooks into an ancient belief of the English that they are in a small country surrounded by bigger tougher neighbours. The story of England and the English is constantly being told as guile and pluck overcoming muscle and unstoppable force, with a dry wit and comic understatement. In truth, this is one big, self-serving, Anglo fantasy.

You can divide humour into two schools. There is Jewish humour and there is English humour. Jewish humour is a comedy of the oppressed. You gain comfort and solace when you have very little direct power. It is the escape of the bullied and is told behind the back of the bully, and it is often self-analytical, self-lacerating, inverted, doubtful and mordant. English humour is far more robust. It's aggressive, bombastic and extrovert. Jewish humour is intimate and personal, English humour loud, gangish and general.

It's notoriously difficult to define humour, but it's broadly true that there is the resistant dry laugh of the bullied, and the cruel guffaw of the bully. English humour is the sound of the bullies. The over-told story of the English underdog overcoming the big man with laughter is simply not true. The English constantly use their humour as an indiscriminate bludgeon. Jokes come one at a time and then gang up on victims, relentlessly pillorying Indians, West Indians, Jews, Gypsies, Scots, Irish, French,

Germans, Essex girls, blondes, Catholics, Hindus, Muslims, gays, Northerners, Southerners, Brummies, yokels, cripples, spastics, epileptics, midgets, lunatics, prostitutes, vicars, the Queen, the unions, Tories, chickens, dogs, donkeys, publicans, the devil and God.

There is hardly anyone who hasn't at some point been slapped with the famous English humour. The bullying and teasing laughs pervade almost every aspect of life. Newspapers are a constant patter of punning headlines, would-you-believe-it human interest stories and columns of unkind personal observation written to raise a smile. The humour of embarrassment and the joy of classroom teasing is a national sport, and its very ubiquity is its open-palmed 'What, us?' defence, because at some point everyone suffers for it. Obviously there's no harm meant. If you only beat up Pakis, you're a racist, but if you beat up everyone, it's only having a laugh. And anyway, they should be able to take a joke.

I do it myself. I have reams of furious letters from Welsh people pointing out that if I'd said what I said about them about blacks or Jews, I'd be prosecuted under the Race Relations Act. In fact they're right, but wrong. The reason I won't make those jokes about Jews and Blacks is because prejudice against them has been all too real and the joke is the excuse for the brick. But no one's actually put on a white hood to torment the Welsh – unless you count Druids. Political correctness and alternative comedy came as a reaction to old, misogynist, racist humour with a broad Lancashire accent and a flat-head full of Brylcreem. But it wasn't really that new or alternative. All it did was change the form, not the rules, and alter the focus. Instead of Pakis and mother-in-laws it became Margaret Thatcher and Liberals. Comedy shifted from something Northerners did to Southerners to being something Southerners did to themselves.

Still, the purpose was bullying and ridicule. There was barely a laugh in England that wasn't at someone's expense, everything and everyone the butt of a joke. The English are addicted to it, to the sound of themselves laughing. Laughter is often the only public emotion they feel comfortable with, and the English laugh differently from other people. Listen to them. It's harsher and louder. It's not a personal expression, but a public affirmation. It's a caw of belonging. Go into any pub and listen to the groups of boys chuckling in circles. It's not a sound you hear anywhere else.

The English teeter on the edge of not being able to take anything seriously. The ability to be solemn or even appropriate, reflective or sad in public, is so uncomfortably embarrassing that they're forced to giggle or snigger. I once asked an oncologist what was people's most common reaction to being told they had cancer. After incomprehension and blank denial, he said, they make a joke. Quite often they go on making jokes till the morphine kicks them across the touchline. He'd worked in hospitals in the States. Americans, he said, went, 'Oh my God, oh my God,' then cried, then prayed. They were then very, very serious and very, very well informed, until they got better or didn't. What was odd was that the English thought they were coping well by never facing the seriousness of their condition or reacting appropriately. 'Laughter is the best medicine,' they'd say with a smile. 'By the way,' added the doctor, 'just in case it happens to you, professional advice – it isn't. A combination of chemotherapy and radiation is mostly the best medicine – after surgery.' Being positive helps, but telling jokes isn't being positive, it's denial, and that's inappropriate. Laughing at mortality doesn't make you look brave and nonchalant, it makes you look as if you haven't understood the question.

Look at the English getting married. Weddings have become one long amateur stand-up routine of stag nights, comedy waistcoats, comic readings and comic socks in church, bawdy photos and the chronic palm-sweating, hellish baiting of the best man's speech. Then a school disco of slapstick and more laughs.

The best man's speech at weddings has grown from being a simple toast to the headlining act in an amateur variety show. There is on the internet a site that has over a thousand best man's speeches with star ratings, presumably awarded by members of the congregation. They are the most awful, scrotum-tightening, desperate screeds of jollity, packed full of coy double-entendres (that as ever only mean one thing). Awful winsome bad taste about the groom's early life, the sad young oaf's comedy of vomit, premature ejaculation, gonorrhoea and prostitutes, drunkenness and shaven testicles, sun-burned bottoms, and all the seaside juvenile horror of English jokes rendered granny-safe with euphemisms. These speeches are crimes against humour, humanity and love.

The English can no longer shed tears for the romance of love, they have to be tears of laughter at the grisliness of sex. The English have lost the ability to bear emotions in front of one another that don't come with a wink. Funerals are full of gags because 'he'd have wanted it that way'. The human condition is an assault course for English jokers because 'you've got to laugh, haven't you?' At its best comedy illuminates darkness, rights wrongs. It really can slay dragons, save lives, capture castles, heal wounds, and bring you closer to the soul of humanity than almost anything else; but only if it lives in a complete range of emotions, if it has a sense of proportion and position and sensibility.

The English are dulled to numbness by their hollow laughter, the constant resort to humour to diffuse and deflate anything that might be painful or complicated. Those old English politenesses of 'keep your chin up, keep smiling, don't forget to laugh, don't lose your sense of humour' have been the comfort and the only solace for millions of broken hearts and bereavements, for misery and disaster. It's a terrible indictment of a culture that is really only comfortable with two public emotions – fury and sniggering. And that's really the point of English humour. An awful lot of it is anger in fancy dress.

It isn't just that a lot of English jokes are subverted anger, or that humour is anger's minder, it's that the jokes and the puns and the comic teasing get the rolling boil of English irritation into places where it wouldn't normally be countenanced. You can be vicious with a laugh where you couldn't without. English comedy is war by other means and it still is the actual last war. The rest of Europe looks on with growing exasperation and incomprehension at the English's ability to endlessly bait the Germans for losing the war and consistently tease the French for losing it as well. It becomes like an embarrassing Tourette's of raised-arm salutes and Dambuster marches. Europeans can't understand the English inability to move on, to get over it. But that's the point. Their reaction, their visible irritation at being called 'a Hun' sixty years later, is what the joke's for. It's supposed to provoke that reaction and this is the fundamental difference between the English sense of humour and that of almost everyone else. Most people share a joke, the English aim them.

A German I know will on occasion tell you his father died in the concentration camps. He waits for the concerned and properly sympathetic faces and then adds that he got drunk and fell out of a watchtower. Europeans find that boorish, faintly crass and rather tasteless; the English love it. It's a proper joke, and a German doing it is double bubble. The surprise is that neither the Europeans nor the English realize that it's not a joke at all, his father really did fall out of a watch tower and it's poignant and sad because his son never knew him, never met his dad.

Football stadiums are the places where you really see the shitty end of the English laugh. People like me, who don't go very often, are always surprised that everyone else seems to know the words to all the songs and when to start and finish. I sat in the terraces at Chelsea and heard the crowd make a hissing noise as the two teams ran onto the pitch. They were playing Spurs. 'Yids,' my neighbour said helpfully. Yes? 'Well, they're North London, Jewish, and, well, it's the noise of the gas going into the ovens, isn't it.' It was so shocking, so astonishingly surreally nothing to do with football, that I laughed and my neighbour smirked. And wagged a finger, 'Got you.' And that's what the English like about a well-aimed joke; they like to make you laugh despite yourself; to make you complicit in something disgraceful. That's the joy, to have your laughter make some toff pillock, some Liberal shirt-lifter a hypocrite.

Football terraces are really, really funny and really, really horrible, both at the same time. It's the volume and the power, the huge wattage of anger, sharpened with a malevolent wit. The monkey noises at black players, the bellows of abuse at anyone who's admitted in passing that they read the *Guardian*; the sing-song repetition of the widely held belief that some bloke's wife takes it up the shitter. The relentless nailing of ugliness, of weakness, of foreignness.

At rich Chelsea, plumbers and kitchen-fitters look over the pitch at Liverpool fans and sing, 'Sign on, sign on, with hope in your heart 'cos you'll never work again.' They wave bulging London wallets at lads down from the north-east, and shout 'Loads of money'. Or they just do cosmic *a cappella* scat-swearing. Anyone who thinks shouting 'fuck and cunt' isn't clever or funny has never been to a football match. The whole ghastly secret, vile, dark laundry basket of young Englishmen's fears, prejudices and braggadocio is tipped out under the floodlights and bellowed at the top of their voices. It's hideous and invigorating and group therapy, and it's like watching a sitcom where the studio audience has all the best lines.

None of this is to say that there aren't finely observed, illuminating or surreal comic writers, performers and blokes in pubs in England, but the collective English sense of humour is mostly a finishing school of bullying, insecurity, jealousy, fear, aspiration and the bonding of young men. Women get the joke and can sometimes tell the joke, but they're exceptions. This English humour is a male thing, and a young male thing. And there's nothing particularly clever (as in difficult) about making other people laugh. It's not science, or medicine or poetry or music. It's not even cooking or woodwork; it's nothing like as difficult as moving them to tears. Comedy is a silly knack, like shuffling cards. Look at the people who do it. Do they look like Nobel Laureates relaxing with a few yuks?

Anyone can learn to do English humour, its dance steps, reactions, situations and statements. As we get older less and less makes us laugh out loud. A joke is like pop music. One day you turn on the radio and realize that nothing is being sung with you in mind any more. You've had your moment at the jukebox and now it's someone else's iPod. Humour is like that – you watch a comedy show and the catchphrases just seem to be stupid and nonsensical. The characters are all revolting and the situations embarrassing, and you begin to think it's everyone else, everyone else's fault that they've lost the humour gene. So you resort to recounting real humour, people who really were funny, and they look at you with a 'whatever' face and you know it's all moved on.

The English sense of humour doesn't need you in the front line; you can retire to wit (a joke that doesn't make you laugh) and irony (a joke that isn't either witty or a laugh). You could even be a self-made part-time wit, take it up as a hobby. So many people have made pin money from after-dinner speaking. It's quite easy – just quote dead people. It's not plagiarism, it's comedy. There's no theft in comedy because there's nothing worth owning. Making the English laugh is pitifully simple. They're all so enormously proud of their vaunted national sense of humour that they'll get it out at the drop of a 'knock-knock'.

In the evening of life, the only thing that really makes them laugh is grammatical errors in public service announcements, and announcers on the wireless pronouncing urethra and Gide wrong. Finally, the English joke attains its purest form – simply the pleasure of finding fault.

7

Cotswolds

Motorways are sagas. The story of man starts as a footprint in the Rift Valley and leads to a track, a trail, a path, a lane, a turnpike, a road, an autobahn, a vapour trail. We got on our hind legs, shaded our eyes and thought, I wonder. We walked out across Africa and have never stopped. Roads are our biography, the lines of our lives, our allegory of the spirit, the metaphor of life. A road is a song, a poem, a movie, an adventure. It's hope, and optimism, and inquisitiveness.

All the motorways out of London have their own particular stories, their atmospheres. They're imprinted with all our journeys. It's always a surprise how quickly you shrug off the huge city, how the suburbs give up with barely a fight and drift into fields. The road to Oxford in February is paved with pheasants. Having survived a season's intense corporate shooting, the handsome cocks saunter down the verges like mad-eyed transvestite pigeons, stupid and careless with a glossy vanity. Above them on each side of the road you can now see red kites hanging with their distinctively swept-back wings and forked tails. In the scrubby motorway waste there are kestrels, or windhovers. Their numbers dropped precipitously in the fifties and sixties, but they recovered to become Britain's most populous bird of prey, thanks entirely to the motorway, whose verges are little nature reserves for kestrels.

Gerard Manley Hopkins called one '. . . morning's minion, kingdom of daylight's dauphin, dapple-dawn-drawn Falcon . . .

how he rung upon the rein of a wimpling wing In his ecstasy!'
Kestrels always make me think of Hopkins, a hovering, shy man
– literature's master of the sprung rhyme who kept his poems
under the bed. He thought 'The Windhover' was the best thing
he ever wrote and dedicated it to Christ Our Lord.

The sound the English countryside makes is Radio Four. It fills
the car with ambient Englishness, that comforting drone of
small information, common sense and reasonable opinions. The
unflustering drama and the blissfully unfunny humour, the
hymns and the pips and the sonorous weather forecast, all mark
the hours of a journey.

As it gets into its stride, the M40 runs through a deep curved
chalk cutting. You turn a long corner and one of the most
beautiful views in England is revealed like a roll of parchment or
a theatrical set, seen through the proscenium of the Chilterns.
It's a long plain of Oxfordshire, that ideal southern English
landscape, an assorted dapple of steeples and copses, hedges,
villages and farms set in the rolling camouflage of fields. Seen
from the arching cantilever of the road with the drone of Radio
Four lapping against the windscreen, you can't help but love the
Englishness of England. Its understated appropriateness, its
humble utility, its many shades of green – it is so exactly what
you want it to be, with a blue sky scudding with lambkin clouds
and the little aeroplanes that fly dauntless loops at the weekends,
those single-prop jobs that Americans call 'dentist killers', but it
could just as well be Spitfires and Hurricanes. As the chalk hills
pull back you lickety-split down into the landscape, and for a
moment it's like driving into a painting or stepping into a film,
and every time I do it I want to turn round and do it again. This
is how England's seen at its best, sealed inside a car, travelling at
speed. Because when you stop and have to get out, that's when
you notice the details. And the English are all in the detail.

Stow-on-the-Wold is the highest town in the Cotswolds, 800
feet up. It's a windy market on the Roman Fosse Way. It's always

been a rich place. The enormous market square once sold as many as 20,000 sheep in a day. The pleasing pale-yellow local stone is endlessly referred to as honey-coloured, though it could easily be piss-stained, or nicotine-smoked. It builds solid, municipal homes for a rich merchant class. When most English towns were still being made of wood and dung, the sheep towns of the high Cotswolds were being turned out in dressed stone. They boast large and ponderously plaque-encrusted churches, comfortable coaching inns and solid exchanges. Stow must have made a fortune out of the Hundred Years War, holding Flemish weavers to ransom. It is an example of the truth that antiquated rural decay looks picturesque, whereas antiquated industrial decay looks squalid.

Stow is now a set for the daytime soap opera of leisure-time England; instead of bleating woolly flocks of sheep, there are bleating woolly flocks of pensioners. On a bright Wednesday afternoon, everyone out on the town can remember Gracie Fields but can't remember where they left their spectacles. Much of rural England is a playground for second childhoods. The retired and newly decrepit have a child-like joy in bright, soft things like pictures of kittens; they love sucky-sweets and holding hands. In general the English make rather good old people, much better than, say, the Americans, who become ridiculous, over-active, drugged-up, surgically enhanced, randy tortoises. English old people laugh a lot. They're always smiling. They do it because at last they've got these brilliant white even teeth and it would seem such a pity to waste them. A busload of old people looks like a window full of fairy tombstones. They smile and they wrap up warm. They love outward-bound clothes, fleeces and waterproof breathable membranes, wool-rich, wrinkle-free, triple-stitched with toggles and clips and detachable hoods. They want to don the futuristic armour of immortality. As their bodies wilt and fray and leak, their coats and trousers remain pin-bright and, in their prime, fit and strident. English old people are admirable, thoughtful, polite, inquisitive, ruminative and easily entertained. What bit of neurological knicker elastic has to snap to make you wake up one morning and say, 'I'll put in my outdoor teeth, call up the pensioner posse and the mini van and we'll go to Stow-on-the-Wold' – just because it's Wednesday and February.

I can't imagine what would drive someone to come to Stow for pleasure. Without hyperbole, exaggeration or over-statement, Stow-on-the-Wold is the worst place in the world. And it's not that I haven't been to some bad places, places that are more dangerous and more despairing, uglier places where people would sell body parts to beg on the streets of Stow. But they are bad places because of politics, war, weather, geography and luck. And they all know they're bad and would love to be better. What makes Stow so catastrophically ghastly is its steepling piss-yellow vanity. It thinks it's a little smug Hobnob stuck in a tin of dog biscuits. Stow knows it's the honey-dipped bollocks.

The ex-market town's business is now antique shops. There are hundreds and hundreds of them, as there are in most of the towns and villages within fifty miles. This is the Vale of Curios. The thickly paned windows in each crooked little shop coyly display one slab of brown furniture restored to a succulent farm-fresh finish; sitting on it will be three unusable bits of early Victorian china of Chinese inclination, and a teddy bear of great age and psychotic hideosity. There will be a set of implements for standing beside a fire and polishing, a Georgian-ish wine cooler with a spider plant in it and, most prominently, a plaque boasting membership of a medieval-sounding guild of merchants – of curios and crafts, chandlers of silver and brass and tastefulness.

Step inside and you'll be met by the smell of beeswax, Senior Service and despair. Also the beady glare of a Reeves pheasant in a cracked glass box. Behind a southern German knee-hole desk there will fit a period, distressed divorcee doing the *Daily Mail* crossword or filling in the Os, Ds Bs and Ps in a Chinese takeaway menu. She has been cast adrift with this flotsam by a bastard of an ex who went bust in Lloyd's and left her with a gloomy cottage, a Labrador with kidney failure and resentment the size of a cheddar cheese. She works here part-time for Nigel, who's never in the shop because he's doing barn conversions with a Polish builder he's secretly in love with. The antiques are knocked up and around by a spliff-dependent Dutch carpenter and his solvent-snorting girlfriend in Cheltenham. The overwhelming sense of the shop is dark brown depression.

You can't look at a piece without thinking of the tears that have been shed over it. The lives that have been trickled and sobbed away in the company of this stuff. The old dolls' houses that reek of musty, miserable, lonely childhoods; the pictures of anonymous fields and buoyant seas that stared out over loveless blameful bedrooms; all the utensils of a Victorian wife worn to blunt, smooth distraction by below-stairs indenture. These antique and junk shops are the reason the old folk all come to Stow. They make a slow, smiley safari, passing from one tickling door to the next, nodding to the well of loneliness behind the desk, whispering over the washstands and whatnots, picking up chamber pots and muttering, 'Only looking.'

The pleasure in this is in the sucking of teeth over prices, although Nigel tries to stymie this by putting the cost in code, but the old folk ask anyway and are told some fantastic figure plucked from the dreams of straitened circumstances. And they say 'Thank you,' and 'I'll think about it', as indeed they will. There's nothing the old like better than the price of things – the higher and more unreasonable the better. The outrage of cost stuffs them with a sensual frisson of pleasure. It reminds them that they had life on the cheap. All their years of black and white and mono fun were virtually given away for pennies. They like to look at the value of the lost and redundant bits of the past –

they had a corner cupboard just like that . . . those Coronation egg cups.

This comes with a mixture of feelings and the secret totting up of the value of their own little home, stained with the Olympic rings of family mugs and the cold touch of mortality. All this stuff was owned and taken for granted by people not unlike them, people who are now dead, and soon they too will be dead. That little table once stood in the hall and was already old when the new-fangled phone was put on it. Here you can just see the ghostly print of the calls of worry and joy, of reassurance and the small instructions of life, that were made over this unimpressive little mahogany and satinwood, demi-loon, cross-banded card table with a hinged top, price: £1,500, £1,200 trade, £700 cash. That wedding-present clock that was watched through early marriage, confinement, school, jobs and promotions, that toasted in New Years, had its hands corrected with a delicate finger every Sunday, was checked against the wireless news and ticked down the years of a widow's long bereavement and is now unregarded and silent – the stilled pendulum of a life. The old look and they know all this. They see that this year, next year, the next bad winter, their votive objects will be in some shop like this, jostling with the furniture of strangers; the bedhead that creaked, the lingering smell of a drawer. They look and see beneath the surface, they trace the nicks and dents with arthritic fingers, a Braille of incident, a moment in the cave painting of the vanished.

Squeezed between the antiques are those imbecilic stores that are devoted to novelty, a word that in *haut* rural England has turned a somersault and means the utterly predictable. Things that have fantasy purposes, holders and covers for stuff that doesn't require holding or covering, things in miniature and utility made embarrassing with embroidered *bons mots*. There's an enamelled sign that brags: 'We're lounging by the pool.' Who thinks up a thing like that? Who makes it? Who decides to sell it? Who buys it? And finally, for whom does it come as a little witty aside or useful household instruction?

Stow is a town that believes everything old is good and everything modern should only be endured if it's either mock or mocked. Old table is better than new table, tea tastes better from old cup than new one, the aesthetics of the past are the benchmark by which we must measure our apologetic attempts at modernity.

There are stocks on the village green. Not the original stocks, of course, but mock-stocks. Put there so that trippers can be photographed next to the utensils of punishment and public humiliation. And of course Stow has more Morris dancers than is either nice, decorous, interesting or necessary. Most summer weekends they caper. The truth of Morris dancers is that their outfits belie their true unpleasantness. They aren't nice people. They have too much hair and are ripe-bellied, twisted, drunk, bellicose, foul-breathed and tongued. They dance the dance of the Moors with its mysterious veils and flashing scimitars that has been Englished into waggled snot rags and whacked broom handles. Whether it attracts the socially irascible or whether the odium of being a Morris dancer turns them into mystic louts with bells on – who knows? Who cares?

The Morris men always draw a crowd, are photographed and laughed at. No one actually likes them. No one would pay to go to a performance of Morrising in the Albert Hall, or buy the CD. It's all too ugly and clunky and stupid, but what people like about it is that it seems to be a fragment of this place. The dancers are living garden gnomes. Stow in the Cotswolds sends its regrets to the future and turns the present into a continual opportunity for retail mourning.

The antique, novelty shops and tea rooms of Stow are really just a front for the true business of the Cotswolds, which is selling off lumps of itself. Property, second homes and country life dreams are the staple money crop of the Cotswolds. Estate

agents' offices are the engines of the economy. The price of a
modest house here is fifty years of an average modest wage. The
cost of a Victorian vicarage with a bit of garden is a sharp gasp
and a humourless guffaw. A manor house with stables and
paddocks, a croquet lawn and swimming pool, is your eldest
daughter's age with five noughts. Living here is something only
people who don't live here can afford to do. This is the
conundrum of every bit of land within two hours of London,
and because the Cotswolds were always rich and Oxford spread
its theological and academic largesse into the surrounding
country, there are more of the sorts of houses that suit the
country fantasies of the new rich and, of course, they then
attract each other. Blenheim, the local vast house and the most
miserably dour gaff in England – an architectural evocation of bi-
polar depression – sits in a Valium landscape that Winston
Churchill suggested was the finest view in the world, but he
probably only ever saw it through the bottom of a cut glass
darkly.

Now it's a Notting Hill gated community. The rest of
Oxfordshire and Gloucestershire is a loose federation of early
retirement windfall, record royalty, media cash and spiv. The
thing that draws this community together is money and the
collective desire to live rural-lite – that is to have lots of horses
but not much manure, to have fields without hay fever, and
country lanes big enough for 4×4s.

None of this seems a particularly bad thing. I really can't see
that a community made out of electronics entrepreneurs,
television personalities and the children of supermarket impres-
arios is *de facto* a bad thing, any more than a countryside
populated by poachers, dry-stone wallers, stick-dressers, milk-
maids and plough boys is an intrinsically authentic good thing.
Country folk who have been born to rural life tend to be pretty
cavalier about green aesthetics; they dump their cars and fridges
willy-nilly, build hideous agri-bunkers, litter the landscape with

rotting piles of turnips the size of meteors and Serbian-style mass sheep graves. If you want to live in a free and democratic country – which I'm assuming you do – then there's no getting around the right of people to do their living where they can afford to. Our wishes will always be tailored by our wallets. Simply living with your mum in a village doesn't give you more of a right to a home than someone who lives with their mum in the inner city.

In the 1970s agriculture accounted for just three per cent of England's GDP. Today it's less than one per cent. For the country within commuting distance of the cornucopia of London, it's less than 0.4 per cent of the economy. Ninety per cent of the English are what the UN now officially call 'urbanized', and that is a good thing. That's progress and education and leisure time and lengthening life expectancy and raised expectations.

Civilization is a word that shares its tap root with civic. The countryside as a separate entity from the city only exists in England as a technically bankrupt wasteland of malpractice, subsidy and subsistence. Here in the Cotswolds the countryside is the outward-bound arm of the interior design business. It's all about the look and the style and the fad. And it's also about maximizing profits: paddocks and swimming pools and pheasant shoots all add to the bottom line and they also employ a lot more people than farming. You're better off being the gardener/driver/loader for a record-label magnate than a tractor driver for agri-business. I just wish that everybody out here would stop pretending that it's all some timeless, unchanging heritage heartland or that it still produces anything anyone wants, except mortgages and dead pheasants. The fields between the estates and the five-acre gardens and the kiddy-bored pony paddocks of the new ruralists are all trim and neat, but there is very little sign of dirty farming or nature. A few sheep in the middle distance keep the grass cut, but there's no muck-spreading, no tractors, no mud, no blokes with overalls and purposeful dogs.

I went for a walk with a friend in the country above Chipping

Norton. The view's rather dull and the walking's irritating, with fences every hundred yards. There are stiles, of course, and sturdy gates, with hard wood arrows pointing out the footpaths and noticeboards asking you to take nothing but photographs and leave nothing but footprints – as if this were the Serengeti. All the hedges have been mechanically trimmed to army haircuts, the fields are silent, there's no birdsong, only crows flop and bluster like torn bin bags. It's a spiritually and practically barren landscape, like a plastic fruit bowl only there for decoration, to be seen from a distance.

The first thing the new ruralists like to do when they get their little plot of weekend Eden is plant trees. If you feel like an interloper, the simplest way to make yourself part of the landscape is to add to it. Trees are good, there's no down side to a tree. They're altruistic, they're Amazonian, they're pristine and primordial, they eat pollution, they're a habitat, they're shade, they stop erosion, people write poems to trees, trees are good and trees get a grant. You're not going to be there to enjoy them, you plant them for future generations.

Organic is the way for the urban new ruralist to really dig in and take over and manipulate the country. For generations agricultural workers and landowners have kept the city at arm's length by saying that it didn't understand country ways; they were patronizing and offensive: city people couldn't work gates, couldn't hold onto litter, couldn't hold onto dogs. To get into the country you had to come as an apologetic supplicant, as a silent guilty novice, and grudgingly the country might accept you as an outsider, a person to be pitied. But the new urban born-again belief in organics makes the incomers born-again ruralists, über-agrarians. It turns out that the country folk were wrong all along – for hundreds of years – not just wrong but stupid and venal, cruel, short-sighted, destructive and culpably wicked. But never mind. Hey-ho. We can show you how to make amends.

Organics has allowed 28-year-old former models and cosmetics PRs married to reality-television producers to know more about the countryside than fifth-generation farmers. It's made the young, blonde and beautiful into missionaries among the ecologically heathen. They complain about what's grown in fields, about carcinogens, intolerances and respiratory tightening and they demand to know what's being sprayed and spread and shovelled. They don't have opinions, they have beliefs – in husbandry, homeopathy and veterinary medicine – and they'll back them all up with a steely insistence, money and a tourniquet-like pressure on the council, the RSPCA and DEFRA who will listen in cowed awe, and act with alacrity because the weight of the momentum of the nation and the wind of climate change are behind the young, bright new ruralists. Hey nonny nonny no.

The new ruralists in the Cotswolds have great, solid kitchens at the centre of their houses. They are their pride and joy, with central islands and breakfast bars and double sinks and marble for pastry and slate in the larder and two freezers and a fridge that makes ice and an oven that costs as much as a time-share in Ibiza with built-in woks and Japanese grills and rôtisseries. It's all very versatile. But there will also be an Aga, because you have to have an Aga in the country, like you have to have an altar in church. The Aga is the beating heart of your home. You can lean against it in winter, it's got a bar for wet socks and you can keep an orphaned lamb in the plate-warming oven – not that anyone gets their socks wet, and they'd have a fit if you tried to dump an ungutted lamb in the oven. The fact is that the Aga is the largest and most expensive manual toaster in the Western world, though it does make excellent toast – which is a shame, because you have a wheat allergy.

The new ruralists' Cotswold kitchen is a statement of intent. Here in the country you need to make your own entertainment, so you put on a dinner party in the barn. A great deal of the pleasure and expectation of the Cotswolds is having the people who live five minutes away from you in town over from their converted vicarage twenty miles away for dinner in the country. Dinner parties are ridiculous and risible sociable gavottes of aspiration and drunken coupling that wear the leitmotif of the 1980s, the decade of conspicuosity. In the city they died of embarrassment, but they're still alive and steaming in the country, because there's absolutely nothing else to do after dark. In fact most of the eighties is still alive and thriving in the country, and the conversation is pretty much as you remember it – staff, schools, money and fornication. The thing about the new urban countryside is that none of it actually happens outside. Country dinner parties are litanies of complaint about the hopelessness and unmanageability of the green stuff, the staff who don't understand the preciousness of your time or the value of your money. The wall-eyed tasteless gardeners who, the moment your back's turned, will have graffitied your environment with scarlet geraniums.

The chief pleasure, once you've settled in to the new countryside, is the availability of so many complaints. Land prices, the exorbitant amount locals demand for some sodden thistle-clogged corner of north-facing land that's good for nothing and 'we want simply to protect the view from the kitchen', or the ubiquity of rough boys or screaming trial bikes racing up and down on Sundays. The countryside grows complaints and grumbles like blackberries and thistle. It's been whingeing and whining since before wattle and daub. The new ruralists pick up an old tune and add new words. The other thing that country dinner parties are for is sex. In fact, the promise of frequent, D.H. Lawrencian coupling with your boots on and lots of guttural swearing is a reason – maybe a subliminal one – for people deciding to spend a great deal of money to spend their weekends here.

The quality and quantity of rural sex is mostly down to horses.

Merely trotting around a paddock is said to frott a Christian monogamist into a howling carnal itch. There is no more illicit sex in the country than there is in the city, there is just more gossip and a lot more wishful thinking. The country-lite does have more ugly sex than the city, simply because there are more ugly people. The other most pressing reason for rural dinner parties is the consumption of drugs. This really is still the 1980s.

The new ruralists smoke stooks of grass and sniffle garrulous lines of cocaine. They also drink. Somehow it doesn't seem so bad for you out in the countryside, but you are three times more likely to be killed or injured on a rural road at night than on an urban one, and the driver is far more likely to speed off and leave you to die in a ditch, because they will invariably be drunk or chemically paranoid. Country society is only bearable if it's maintained with a thick mulch of the mutually exclusive binary cocktail of mood-altering substances and massive motorcars.

Finally, you're more likely to be killed by a 4×4 than by any other type of vehicle. The bottom line about Oxfordshire and the Cotswolds is that for anything other than a long weekend, it is screamingly, weepingly, head-bangingly boring. The regressive transformation from civilized urbanity to bucolic slack-jawed simplicity is only possible if you manage to embrace the euphemisms of tedium: stillness, silence, thoughtless reverie, rocking, ambling, carrying a stick, talking to yourself, staring into space with your flies open, sleeping in chairs, dribbling – and constant thoughts of suicide.

The countryside isn't a destination in the lifestyle of the new ruralists, it's a pit stop, a tick on the avaricious must-do list of upward mobility. They come and try on the countryside like yoga or the alpha course or the rhubarb-and-horseradish diet. It's an experience that, after a bit, when the kids have got bored with the pony and the quad bike and yearn to spend weekends in clubs in Hoxton and beg for holidays in Ibiza and Kenya, the new ruralists look at the dripping view and the smoky chimney and the infuriating gardener, and listen to the dentist pilots ply the leaden sky, and they have a sudden un-revelation – something cracks. The Aga looks like a big ugly toaster and they think, sod it, let's cash in for a converted olive farm in Chiantishire . . . or a beach house in Barbados . . . or let's just keep the money and rent yachts . . . only let's not sit in the blustery gloom and over-stuffed fug and druggie-ugly sex of the Cotswolds any more. So they hand the vicarage with the swimming pool to a new family for a tidy sum. They reap as they have sown. It is the harvest festival of property.

And the new wannabe ruralists look at it all with round eyes of wonder and see themselves in wax jackets and corded lamb's-wool sweaters, all tousled and pink-cheeked, sucking in the clean air and eating eggs from their own chickens – a boiled egg from the bottom of your own Miss Henny Penny is worth a million pounds of anyone's money. They look at the fat, rheumy-eyed arthritic Labrador and think, we could get a puppy, a pony, a rabbit. They smell the cinnamon and the pale wood smoke and the lavender potpourri and they imagine the sex, and they say, 'Yes, yes, yes,' to the country and this place, this ancient bit of old heritage greenery that has no innate purpose but to be the backdrop for some part-time fantasy. It's a second-hand porn mag, passed from hand to hand, leered at, fingered, wanked over and then passed on.

The structure of the rural countryside is fractured out of sync. It ceased to be a coherent place with a purpose. The old owners pack up the 4×4, drive off down the crunchy gravel along the familiar lanes with their double-barrelled village signs and get onto the road that leads to the motorway, and as they pass through the chalk cutting with the great view of Oxfordshire and the Chilterns behind them without a glance in the rearview mirror, they burst into peals of laughter. It's the laugh of relief at the end of a fairy story, when you wake up to find it's all been just a dream.

8

Sorry

England's default setting is anger: lapel-poking, Chinese-burning, ram-raiding, street-shouting, sniping, spitting, shoving, vengeful, inventive rage. But many of the traits and tics that make the English so singular and occasionally admirable are the deflective mechanisms that they've invented to diffuse anger. The tolls and speed bumps and diversions of anger. Not giving in to your nature is very English, clinging on, white-knuckled, bottling the urges, refusing to slide into spittle-flecked release of snarling national fury.

The simplest and most straightforward way to replace the pin is an apology. The S-word. Eskimos, they say, have dozens of words to describe snow. The Japanese have any number to differentiate rain, the French have a mouthful of facial expressions for 'I don't care what you think' and the Italians a fistful of hand gestures for exclamation marks, and the Welsh have five glottal stops for 'I must have left my wallet with my other wife'. But the English, who have by far and away the largest, biggest, most immense, enormous, vast, gigantic, walloping, king-sized, voluminous, thumping, whacking, macroscopic, megalithic, lusty humdinger of a vocabulary available to any human voice-box, choose to go the other way around and pack meaning into one word.

It was an American who pointed out to me the many subtle and contradictory back-handed and double-dealing ways the English manage to staple onto saying the S-word. He had noticed the light and airy sorry that the middle classes hailed him with when they committed some social infraction, said with a rising and falling inflection like a speed bump negotiated by a Bentley. Sorr-ee.

There are many, many ways of saying sorry. Being English is having to learn how to say all of them. There is: sorry, I apologize; sorry, I don't apologize; sorry, you can take this as an apology, but we both know it isn't one; sorry, will you shut up; sorry, empathy; sorry for your loss; sorry, I can't hear you; sorry, incredulity; sorry, I don't understand you; sorry, you don't understand me; sorry, excuse me; sorry, will you hurry up; sorry, I don't believe you; sorry, I'm interrupting; sorry, this won't do; sorry, I've reached the end of my patience; sorry, sad and pathetic – as in, sorry excuse or sorry little man. You can probably identify more variations on sorry. Sorry is a prophylactic word. It protects the user and the recipient from the potentially explosive consequences of the truth.

Being able to apologize without meaning it, without therefore losing face, but at the same time allowing the other person to back down, having got their apology, is a masterfully delicate piece of verbal engineering.

The English have arrived at a way of being furious without being rude. If you listen to them complain in shops or restaurants or about service in general, they almost invariably start with 'sorry'. You know that a customer sending back his soup, saying 'sorry' this isn't very nice, isn't apologizing and the waitress replying, 'I'm sorry you didn't like it' isn't either. If you speak English as a native tongue, you decipher these nuances without thinking. If you've learnt the language abroad, or don't speak it very well, then you just think the English are cringingly, obsequiously apologetic all the time and are possibly the politest people in the world.

The only other word that comes with so many meanings is 'fuck'. And if you don't understand the incredibly fine and expressive definitions of that – from explosive pain, to happy surprise, to simple punctuation – then you might also imagine that the English are contrarily at the same time the rudest people in the world. And as it happens, both assumptions are true.

9

Animals

Best beloved. The English are kind to animals. It is written in stone and in fur, and they get very, very angry with anyone who says they're not. When God was handing out human traits to make up the characters of all the nations, the English barged their way to the front of the crush with a sense of entitlement, snapping at the lesser countries. And God said, in his infinite, kindly and faintly irritatingly way that there was no need to push, there'd be plenty of traits to go round – except rudeness, which the English already seemed to have got, and everybody tittered. And the English blushed and sulked, and went and looked at the bookcase and said they really weren't that interested.

And when everybody got all the traits they could carry and were chattering gaily and swapping and admiring each other's national adornments and gaudy psychology, God went over to the English and put his hand on their shoulder and said, 'Come on, there are still some lovely traits left. Choose a couple.' And the English shrugged their shoulder and glanced at what was left. 'How about hospitality to strangers?' said God. And the English made a snorting noise. 'Why on earth should we be nice to that dago rabble?' 'Well, what about kindness to children?' The English harrumphed, and said, 'Spare the rod.' 'Well, here's artistic? And convivial? What about devout?' God said, hopefully. But the English rolled their eyes and said, 'Look, awfully good of you and all that, but we really don't think that this business is us.' 'But you've got to take something,' said God. 'Oh well, if you insist. We might just take a pet. That poor neglected little thing in the corner – we'll have kindness to animals.' 'Really?' said God. 'Do you think that's enough to build a whole national character on?' 'Oh, plenty', said the English. 'Just you see what we can make out of this.' And with a strange, humourless little smile they tucked kindness to animals under their arm and marched home.

I was once in Luxor. On street corners there were little awnings, like tall bus stations. They had signs on them boasting that they'd been built for the comfort of the local horses and paid for by a committee called something like the Committee for the Relief of Sadly Abused Egyptian Horses, Patron Princess Agatha Maud of Leinster, or someone very similar. There were any number of horses and they all looked as if they could do with a bit of relief – skinny, splay-footed things with ribs like xylophones and worn, calloused hips, bony knees and backs like Scottish glens. They struggled in the biblical heat to do the bidding of men in nighties, who whipped them till their tongues lolled – the horses, not the men – and their withers were flecked with blood and froth.

At crossroads you'd often see them collapsed in the traces, unable to take another step; sunk to bloody knees, their drivers belting and kicking them with incandescent frustration. Then others, blocked in their paths, would come up and offer boots and blows until the horse would disappear in a flay of Egyptian rage. After a few satisfying moments, a wiser head would prevail and someone would come forward and shout at the kicking and beating men, usher them away, and give them a bit of a lecture in Egyptian – presumably on self-control and common decency. He would examine the nag, pop something into his mouth, chew for a few moments ruminatively, and then remove a sticky wad and with surprising speed and dexterity jab it into the rolling eye of the beast, who would give a whinny of utter agony and, with the last vestiges of existence, scrabble and stumble to its feet, sweating under the yoke of its worldly lot, head rolling in pain. And the bystanders would laugh and clap. Aah, a wad of tobacco in the eye, the most painful thing known to man or animal, what a blessing.

The driver would smile and shake the man's hand before leaping back onto his laden cart, giving the horse a wallop, and staggering off about his business. All this I have seen. More than once. And if you go to Luxor, I'm sure you could see it. There are fewer and fewer horses now, of course, because local business-men would rather have a Toyota truck. But there are still abused nags for the edification and comforting sadness of visitors. Most of them do what most of them have always done – work twenty hours a day, pulling the little taxi cabs for tourists, most of whom are English, this being Egypt, and Egypt being rather an English place.

The horse shelters made me think a number of things – none of them about Egyptian horses. Firstly, how would we like it if county towns were suddenly enlightened with little huts for the comfort of homesick English children, donated by the Egyptian Committee for the Alleviation of Boarding-School Unhappiness, Patron Abdul someone or other? I thought how understanding and long-suffering the other nations of the world are in accommodating the finger-wagging patronage and bullying, blind rudeness of the English, and I thought that being kind to animals is only peripherally about animals. Its pleasure and its real purpose is to be unkind to people.

It is an empirical truth that collectively and individually the English are no kinder to animals than anyone else is. Their continental nickname, *rosbif*, indicates that at least cows could question their sympathy for God's creatures. They race dogs and horses, eat everything with a cardio-vascular system – except dogs and horses – shoot birds imported and bred for the purpose, wear leather and feathers and drown just as many kittens as anyone else. The RSPCA, an organization that is peculiarly English, has a Royal Warrant, whilst the NCPCC, that does much the same thing for human children, doesn't seem to merit one. The RSPCA is a semi-official police force that dresses up in prison officer's uniforms and takes people to court for collecting birds' eggs and torturing prawns. It is one of the richest charities in the country. It has a fundamental born-again political agenda when it comes to dumb creatures. It regularly produces research showing that, despite their best efforts over dozens and dozens of years, and having spent millions and millions of pounds, cruelty to animals continues to get worse. They arrange with the police to film suffering animals for the shocked edification of the public, and you don't need to have been in England for a week to work out that they really aren't in the animal kindness business, they're in the animal cruelty business. The more cruelty the better. The greater the need for the RSPCA, the larger the charitable donations. So they spend a great deal of money ferreting out and publishing four-legged misery.

The most unpleasant and viciously unreconcilable terrorists in the world are the very English animal liberationists who sadistically target humans who keep guinea-pig farms or catteries. The level of violence and malevolence directed at these people, at their children, their neighbours and bystanders, is unmatched by anything in the Old Testament, or anything the finest Latin-American nihilist guerrillas have ever come up with.

Kindness to animals gives the English not just a licence but an obligation to hound and dog those whom they deem to be less than perfect in their relationship with fluffiness. When it comes to animals, the Taliban look like social workers in comparison with the English. The brilliance of this orthodoxy is that if you have the God-given right to speak on behalf of animals, then no one can gainsay you. The critters are dumb with gratitude and you are well known for your kindness to them, which allows you to be simply vile to anyone you choose. Only in England is it a cliché worn smooth with over-use to say, 'I think I prefer animals to people.' You can even specify a species: I think I prefer dogs . . . horses . . . salamanders . . . to people. The utter moral bankruptcy, the appalling dereliction of human responsibility or interest implicit in this statement is taken as a given by large swathes of the country.

I may be putting the cart before the horse, the chicken before the egg. The English love of animals may not be because it gives them an excuse to patronize, bully and be psychotically spiteful to other people, it may be because they are incapable of being open, friendly and honest with other people. Have the English ever needed an excuse to be appalling? The vast speechless instinctive realm of nature gives the English the great toy box and analyst's couch for their thwarted, stunted and twisted social emotions; and they admit as much. Live amongst the English for a year and you're bound to hear from someone that 'dogs are much more straightforward than people, you know' or 'he gives me uncompromising loyalty'. Loyalty in England is a trait that is reserved exclusively for animals and Gurkhas. You will hear women talk about their cats in terms that the rest of the world saves for private conversations about lovers, and men will admit that, whilst they haven't shed a tear since their mother left them at the school gates, they cried like stricken toddlers when they had to have the old Labrador put down.

One of the many roles the English take on with regard to the rest of the world in general and each other in particular, is that of the wronged lover, without there ever having been an affair, or indeed any intimation of affection. The English behave as if the rest of the world is in breach of promise, that they've been dumped, and they can retreat with wounded hearts, muttering that it is better that they loved and lost, and that they can turn their abused emotions onto the animal kingdom, who will love them back. The English have an insatiable bottomless lust for nature in all its manifestations, but particularly on television. If you ask them what they think the Almighty will be like when they get to heaven, most of them will say David Attenborough.

It is in the nature of TV and the nature of nature on TV that it comes with a plot, a narrative and a purpose. And that's what the English like most. They can overlay the instinctive action and reaction, the hard-wiring of animals with order that allows them to be good and kind and clever and important – that's the English, not the animal.

Perhaps the greatest of English artistic talent is their masterful skill and inventiveness when it comes to anthropomorphism. They can see a sense and rough order in nature that is missing in human society. It is kindly, cruel, efficient and miraculous in a way that human society never manages to live up to. The English can cover nature with their own blanket of sentimentality and create a world the way they want it to be, not to be part of it, but to oversee it, to be custodians. When God allowed the English to take away 'kindness to animals', what they knew he had given them was permission to play God. It's often said that the English think that God is an Englishman – that's as maybe – but this doesn't fully comprehend the English position. This is that the English are as one with God, that the problems are caused by atheists and heretics, and that if the rest of the world understood that in fact the English were a deific people and the custodians of creation, then everything and everyone would be much happier. It's worth bearing in mind that the defining characteristics of fascists and psychopaths are great sentimentality combined with amoral cruelty.

If you really wanted to see the depth of the deformity of the English relationship with nature, then you should go to Cruft's – the largest, oldest, most venerable dog show in the world. Saying that is like the Americans claiming to run a baseball World Series. Only Americans and those imitating Americans play baseball, and only those with some weird desire to imitate the

English would possibly want to have the world's biggest dog show.

Cruft's sports an absurd and terrifying variety of dog. The unique skill of canines has always been that they're really good at mutating, very fast. They are the McDonald's of the animal kingdom. This ensures that as a genus they have done very well by being the Englishman's bitch. More breeds of dog have been created and classified by the English than by all the other humans in the world put together. In a dog the English have found their perfect partner; they can breed it to be everything they have found wanting in people, every nuance of behaviour that could be mistaken for character can be bred into dogs. The great asset the dogs have in all this is that being pack animals, they learn behaviour by minutely watching how other dogs further up the hierarchy behave; so by watching the English very, very carefully, the dogs turn themselves into perfectly little furry Englishmen.

The wild dogs of Africa, *Lycaon pictus*, are the most efficient of all the great African carnivores. They have a hunt-to-kill ratio of something close to 90 per cent. They are long-distance chasers. Once the pack locks onto a quarry, they will run it down with a relentless single-minded determination. When they eventually run it to exhaustion, one dog will grab a nose or lip, and another a tail or rump, and the third and fourth will then eviscerate it. The pack feeds with a famished violence. English game wardens and farmers in the early twentieth century had a concerted policy of genocide for wild dogs. They tried with an equally long-term marathon determination to wipe them out. Not because they were a danger to people or livestock, but because they were an abomination; they were deemed too cruel to be allowed into the Englishman's creation. They didn't conform to the rules of a perfect English world. Having created thousands of breeds of dog, the English felt perfectly at liberty to exterminate one on the grounds of sentimental eugenics.

The real sadness of the English trait of caring for animals is that, having purposefully dissociated themselves from their own species, they don't have an integrated equal relationship with nature. Their anthropomorphism and unrequited love set them apart from the objects of their desire. The truth is that the natural world doesn't give a fig for the English. It has no plot, no narrative, there is no happy ending to nature, there is no heaven of happy dogs and horses reunited with their owners. If the English were made extinct tomorrow, not a single dog in the world would care, because caring is not in their nature. They'd look and learn to be someone else, and somewhere deep inside the English know this. They may be weird, anthropomorphizing, sentimental, repressed monsters, but they're not stupid.

10

Drink

I am an alcoholic. I remember my first drink; first drinks are important to alcoholics. They're the start of something big, something life-changing. It's where you earn your other name, your appellation, your label, your vintage. Mine is 1969, my first unsupervised drink. I'd been given watered wine by my parents because that's what they did in France, and France was the gold standard for civilized table life, and my grandmother would slip me tiny crystal glasses of ginger wine at Christmas. The glasses were cut to look like thistles – I liked them more than the wine. My first real drink, the drink that did it, was at boarding school in the fields that rolled out from behind our cricket pitch – a bottle of cider and a quarter bottle of English cooking brandy. I was fifteen and everything was happening very fast: sex, cigarettes, politics, books, arguments and the terror of the life waiting to be lived.

I remember adolescence as like being put on a horse at the start of the Grand National and told that if you fell off at the first jump, the options for the rest of your life would be reduced to waiting tables. As I'd tried waiting tables in the holidays and found it beyond me, I was properly scared. It would be neat to say that that first throat-tightening mouthful of drink flicked a switch, that a light went on and change occurred at a molecular level, but I don't remember it like that. A week later I badgered a friend to walk the mile and a half to the Fox in the village of Willian to buy a surreptitious under-age half of Guinness served out of the back window and drunk with a disproportionate glee. Why Guinness? God knows. Why walk a three-mile round trip in the dark, across open country, for a half pint? That's not normal. But then nothing you do is normal at fifteen. Everything is plagiarized, borrowed or made up out of nothing. Your life's like a Third World gift shop, you keep trying to guess what the rich grown-ups want in the hope that one day you'll become one of them. What I do remember is that drink cut the edge off the fear of failing at life before I'd even started living.

I wasn't any good at academic work, there was no natural path for me to university, my family didn't have a business or a farm or an hereditary connection to the Armed Forces that I could slot into. The twentieth century had given us a liberal disposition and the freedom to make of our lives what we could, and at fifteen that was a prospect so terrifying that I would lie awake at night rigid with the misery of great expectations – and a drink, or several, took that and folded it up and made it manageable. It expanded me and reduced everything else. It was the Gulliver option.

There are problems with starting to drink. The first being, it's horrible. Alcohol is nasty stuff, your throat naturally tries to reject it, it burns, it tastes horrid. You have to force yourself to drink, like smoking. That's frightful too, but actually drink helps with that. To begin with you don't drink for the thousands of subtle notes in a vintage, or the hoppiness, the barleyness, the grapey, toasty, leathery, flowery euphemism of drink. You drink to get drunk. Kids are very straightforward about drinking, and we drank like aborigines. We sat on benches under trees, in cowpat fields, hugging ourselves, passing bottles and cigarettes and wet kisses and laughter, waiting for it to work. And it certainly worked for me.

Alcoholics' stories are narratives. They rise and fall with drama, humour and pathos. They're descriptive and emotional, they're sagas and parables. We tell them to each other a lot; they get polished and improved, and if you're hearing one that isn't slurred and burped or told with self-pity and anger you're probably listening to a happy ending. The point is that they have a plot, but the plot is always retrospective. It's a trail that becomes obvious after you've travelled it. While you were living it there is no plot, no plan, no goal, no grand design. The one thing you should always bear in mind about drink is that all drunks are different, in the same way, and that nobody, absolutely nobody ever picked up a drink thinking it would make their day worse.

The English have a huge drink problem. Their one consolation is that it might not be quite as bad as the Scots and the Irish problem. In America, alcoholism is sometimes referred to as the Celtic disease, but actually the whole world has a drink problem. It's hard to find a country where a great many of the social ills aren't related to drink or drugs, particularly in the ones that are dry or have prohibition. To say that humanity has a problem with drink and would be better off not doing it is like saying it has a problem with sex or the weather. It just is the way we are, it's what we do, it's our recreational weather. But for some people it seems to be sunnier than for others, and whilst all societies drink, they don't all drink the same. The northern nations have a particular affinity to scrappy oblivion, but even in cold Europe the English stand out as being particularly crap drunks.

Bad is a value judgement that has an alternative view: if the point of drinking is to get drunk and release inhibition, then actually, the English are very good at drinking, but drink is still a constant and major social problem. It's the gravest social problem – one in four hospital beds is occupied by someone with a drink-related or exacerbated condition. Almost all domestic violence and violent crime is committed with the help of a drink. Drink is a major contributor to accidents and absentee-ism. In fact it's difficult to find a social ill from unwanted pregnancy and sexually transmitted diseases to carpet-chewing club bores and single-issue obsessives that doesn't have 'just the one' at its heart. And of course, drink kills you. It takes years off your life and is the guide of your terminal illness.

In Amsterdam a prostitute once asked me why the English were such awful drinkers. She'd had a singular opportunity to study Europe's drinking habits. Italians, she said, were charming drunks, the French pretentious, the Spanish dark and self-destructive, the Germans pretended they weren't drunk, the Dutch were morose and apologetic, the Scandinavians incomprehensible, then comatose; but the English, the English were hideous, violent, foul. They came in groups, they'd swear and bully, they didn't want to pay, they all wanted to have a go for the price of one; then they were too drunk to do it, and then they'd blame the girls and they'd get violent. 'Why are they like that?' she asked. It was obvious that she had seen in drink caricatures of accepted, national characteristics. Charming Italians, pompous French, violent English.

For the English, drink is the key that unlocks the cellar door to their dark side. Whilst it may heighten and enlarge the national characters of their neighbours, it doesn't do quite the same for the English. Their character is built on, and devoted to, subduing their nature.

An Englishman is a series of restraints and bandages, straps, patches, plasters, muzzles, hair-shirts and rubber underwear; all self-imposed for restraining, hiding and controlling the id. It wouldn't be the whole truth to say that drink unlocks the inner Englishman, that in vodka there is veritas, because the true nature of the English is their struggle to contain and smother a large section of their raw inclination. The English are high-maintenance, self-imposed people. The idea of a real Englishman is almost a contradiction in terms, like talking about a real theme park, or a real golf club. All the people of cold northern Europe put great store on controlled drinking, at being able to handle or hold drink, which essentially means being able to maintain your front. Drinking becomes an exercise in brinkmanship.

As with so many things that ought to be intuitive relaxed fun, the English impose a great many rules on drinking. If they didn't quite invent French wine, then having been the greatest consumers of it since the Hundred Years War they invented and refined the classification and snobbery of it. Few things are quite as English as the minute listing and grading of wine. The whole paraphernalia of wine-drinking is very English. Naturally the French, being partial to a nip of snobbery, took to it with alacrity. But it's the northern societies that invented drinking games, the ritual of rhyme and forfeit, the childish repetitions in hot smoky rooms.

The English don't stipulate how much you should drink, just that you shouldn't exhibit any of the effects of drink. Being a good drinker is not about indulgence or pleasure, it's about resisting drink – whilst drinking. And then there are hangovers. The English are enormously partial to hangovers. An Italian once told me he thought that the English drank specifically to get hangovers. He said they seemed to take to them with great pleasure. They will come down to breakfast holding their heads and groaning gleefully. They'll eat huge quantities of appalling fried food and make special patented concoctions involving eggs and chillies and the bottled proprietary condiments that England has such a bewildering variety of. They take such evident pleasure in being invalids and being able to play both doctor and patient, pampering themselves and wallowing in the pain and the misery, swearing they'll never do it again, re-living with excruciating embarrassment the behaviour of the night before. I have never seen the English enjoy themselves as much as when they can collect around a shared hangover.

Alcoholics divide drunks into two sorts: topper-uppers and binge-drinkers. I was a topper-upper. I started drinking at fifteen and by the time I was nineteen I was drinking every day and continued to drink every day, come sickness or prohibition, until I was poured into a treatment centre at the age of thirty. I was, in English terms, very good at drinking. Too good. I had a capacious capacity for absorbing the stuff and had worked out the Dumb Crambo of moving around when your internal gyroscope has fallen over. I learned to enunciate when my mouth felt like it was made out of putty, and my teeth had all changed places and I had the tongue of the dog whose hair I'd consumed. I drank steadily, with a steely determination. I drank on and through peripheral neuritis, alcoholic gastritis, an atrophied brain, an enlarged liver, a damaged pancreas, black-outs, suicidal depression, anonymous bloody sores and DTs so severe that I would have to take the first drink of the morning using a towel hooked round my neck as a pulley, because I was frightened of knocking my teeth out with the glass.

I went for help one April, and the doctor who gave me the once-over said that I'd better be serious about stopping, because if I didn't I was unlikely to see another Christmas. Incredulous friends said they couldn't believe I had a problem as they'd never seen me drunk. The truth was, they'd never seen me sober, I'd just woven drink into the fabric of who I was and I had to unpick it.

Unravelling your life when you've no other life is not easy or pleasant, and I don't recommend it, unless you need to, and then I can't recommend it enough. Being a topper-upper meant that when I was finally told I was an alcoholic, I saw in a flash the bald, sad truth of it. There was little 'get' out of that room, the choice was to continue alcoholic drinking or stop. Binge-drinking is different. Binge-drinkers can go days, sometimes weeks without drinking. When they do drink, though, they go for it; they will drink to oblivion and beyond, and the binges will get longer and the periods between shorter and more remorseful.

It's binge-drinking that is the English calamity. Not just bingeing individuals, but bingeing communities. Anyone who's been through a market town on a Friday night will have seen the violent, chaotic, staggering state of hundreds of kids. Drunkenness is their key to companionship, belonging, sex, laughter and an intensely good time, and that is the driving ambition, the Holy Grail and the really addictive drug of choice of young England. It's not the drink, it's that great bonding, brilliant moment of bright, elevating, hugging, glorious, risk everything, timeless happiness that makes everything else worth it.

The corrosive, self-destructive, embarrassing dead-end behaviour that is the bill they pay in pursuit of the great clan joy has been part of English life for as long as the English have been an identifiable people. When the state and the editorials look at the pandemic of bingeing in young people, they invariably see it as a problem, because from the sober standpoint it is. And they ascribe this to any number of social deficiencies – the breakdown of families, the lack of alternative entertainment, the paucity of education, the absence of work, the ugliness of environment, the cheapness of drink, the culture of inebriation. And all or any of those things may be true, but they're not the truth.

Young England's relationship with drink isn't their problem, it's their *raison d'être*. The booze and bonking holidays that so disgust southern Europe and embarrass provincial England are ardently worked-for and dreamed-of. The multiple partners, the vomiting, the hideous sunburn and bruises, the police cells, the grim hotels, the airport hell – it's not a nightmare, it's an English dream. They don't do it because something's wrong, they'll put up with loads that's wrong so they can have this. On Friday nights and stag nights and for two weeks in the summer, this bingeing is what's utterly brilliant about being young and English.

On the other side of drunkenness there is a no less committed balance of prohibition and abstinence in England. My great, great uncle, who had drunk the farm by the time he was thirty, signed the pledge and lived a white-knuckle strait-laced exist-ence ever after. The rise of Methodism and the dissenting chapels and the great Victorian social reformers all grew out of the monster drink. Vast amounts of energy and money and effort were poured into separating the Englishman from his bottle. The proposed remedies have changed very little over the centuries – making the stuff more expensive, offering leisure alternatives and spiritual fulfilment via teetotalism. This, by the way, is one of the very few English words to be based on a speech impediment. A religious zealot for abstinence would hold public meetings to harangue the workers about drink. There were two flavours of abstinence – abstinence from spirits that allowed the consumption of beer, and the hard-line total abstinence. Unfortunately, our man had a rather severe stammer, and when his public meetings were recorded by journalists, undoubtedly not entirely sober ones, they reported his impediment literally, and total abstinence became teetotal.

Over the century the reforming, straight-living, hard-working, good-book-and-cocoa social improvers may have changed indi-vidual lives, but they've had comfortingly little effect on the drinking habits of society and specifically on the young. If you were designing a rational, smoothly functioning, sensible and healthy nature from scratch, then top of your list of things to pan would be no alcohol. It has very little to commend it. Simply fiddling with its presentation or cost is going to make little difference. Drink isn't a stain on the English character, it is the founding dedication of young England's character. They drink because they can. It isn't a mistake, it isn't a symptom, it's a huge pleasure. And despite what the Italians and Dutch prostitutes and anyone else might think, the English are very, very good at it.

11

Gardens

Seen from 1,000 feet above, England's most striking feature is its greenness. England rolls out under you like a quilt of motley. But stand on its face and England looks like a hugger-mugger suburb. At ground level there is barely room to swing a vista. Above, it all seems to have been stitched together by a victim support group, a personal and slightly dotty act of memory, mourning, make do and mend. It's surprising how much of this island is still dedicated to nature. You also notice how many astonishingly hopeful swimming pools there are. The only thing the English are optimistic about is the weather. Towns and cities look like grey islands in a stained glass sea of green connected by a web of road and rail that elegantly picks its way round the contours of real rural England.

The green greening greenwood, greensleeves, green belt, green wellies, greengage, green cross, green room, green house, green-fingered nature of England is its abiding legend. Its central parable. England is at heart and hearth in its collective self-belief a *country* country. This green and pleasant land. The urban is the aberration, the bald patch in the verdant growth. England has no creation myth, there's no event or person from which the idea of nation germinates. 1066, famously the only nationally known date, was the beginning of a new volume of an already old story. The Normans beat the Danes, who were themselves invaders.

It's easy to see England's story as a series of new beginnings and fresh starts, a collation of continental overtures. This litany of family story begotten of invasion, so beloved of Churchill and lyric poets and prep-school teachers, is a shorthand convention, a shuffle of the history card that draws attention away from the embarrassing fact that there is no obvious start to England – either geographically or socially. Romulus and Remus are absent, there is no Homeric legend, no Nordic fairy story of giants and gods. Before England was a political entity it was a religious one, but neither St Augustine nor Bede, nor the village-naming saints of the West Country, are fathers of the nation. King Arthur is almost an English Daddy hero, but his appeal was always more intellectual and bohemian than popular. Arthurian legend is just too weird and troubadourishly French for Anglo-Saxon literalism. He might have inspired the painters and poets of Chelsea but he never really played the back-to-backs of Sheffield. And it's the same with Beowulf, who wasn't English at all. The closest England came to having a do-it-all hero was the first Ombudsman – Robin Hood. A properly popular bloke whose myth still speaks to much in the English.

Robin Hood in his Lincoln green is the evocation of an older, deeper silent keeper of England, Hern the Hunter, the green man. Here we are back at the green. Before going any further into the greenwood in pursuit of the green man, we should remember the very English habit of garden-shed mystical saga-spinning, do-it-yourself, antiquarian pixilation. Because of the absence of creation myth, and particularly because of their horribly repressed imaginations, there is a long and ghastly history of Englishmen who invent fairytales and hedgerow fantasies about the oldie-fairy world. Blokes with pipes and unique hats who collect folk songs and folklore, who rediscover or resurrect dark-age festivals and runic sagas. The eighteenth and nineteenth centuries were particularly replete with this stuff, as was inter-war Oxford. There was a sort of national envy for the glamorous and extravagant mythologies that lesser nations were able to boast. And there was a need to create a source of nationalism and destiny. Folklore in all its capering, bell-strung, well-dressing, cheese-rolling, wicker-burning, blushing, floral gaudy is the ancient English hobby. Folklore owes more to sour cloudy beer drunk from pewter tankards in a suburban snug than it does to any real popular culture or heritage.

The great, infallible test of popular culture is always 'Is it popular and is it culture?' and if the answer to either of these is no, then it probably never was. But the green man may be, though few people could now place him or know who he was. Shakespeare writes about Hern the wild huntsman in *The Merry Wives of Windsor*, a romping proto-farce written at the instruction of Queen Elizabeth, who wished to resurrect a dead Falstaff. He may well have reminded her of the nicer aspects of her father.

Falstaff has become a totemic English father figure. Hern only gets a passing mention, but this was at a time when England needed to assert a strong sense of its identity. He is the ghostly huntsman who protects certain forests with a pack of spectral hounds. His appearance is neither necessarily good nor evil, just often chaotic and contrary.

Green is the colour of magic and spells, and the green man now is most commonly seen as a pub sign, but his face appears carved into the ornate masonry of medieval cathedrals. It's a puckish face, spewing tendrils and buds of plants, whose hair curls into leaves, who seems to breathe suckers and shoots. He's half man and half tree, but he's not altogether clear if he's flesh becoming vegetable or vegetable becoming human. He is subtly both a corruption and a rebirth, potency and death. He is the ancient English spirit, and it is his nature to be camouflaged, to remain hidden in the dapper dapple of the wood.

The green man is a spirit who inhabited the great deciduous forest that stretched from Southampton to the Caledonian pines of Northumberland. The original old England was wooded, a place of secret glades and darkness. Forest people have a more ambivalent and mysterious relationship with nature than pastoralists. The forest is gone now; the English cut it down and grew in its place a landscape of their own design, in their own blunt image. The country you see from 1,000 feet has the aspect of an eternal truth, the embodiment of a gifted, perfect England, but it's a nouveau landscape, a fake antique. Few but the most ruggedly folksy would recognize the green man in England's life now. But you can see the life and the belief that first created and nurtured him all around you. He is the spirit of gardening. Puck. The hobbit of the garden. The sprite of the window box and the hanging basket. The tender of the grass verge and the municipal floral clock, the memorial garden and the water feature. No people on earth have taken to gardening like the English, except perhaps the Japanese, whom the English resemble more than they would like to think.

Gardening is the great English cultural expression, far truer to their nature than novels, plays or poetry. Gardening is the English spirit. It's into the soil that they bury their prejudice and snobbery. The garden is England's great contribution to civilization. It's difficult to imagine what could have started off gardening. You can't think of a scenario where a peasant comes home from toiling in the fields and says, 'Hey, there's still a couple of hours of daylight left. I think I'll do some digging for fun and grow stuff we can't eat.' Almost certainly gardens in Britain began with the Church. The Romans may have imported flowers, but gardens as we understand them came from monasteries. The word comes obliquely from 'ghor', meaning enclosure. An enclosed monastery garden, maybe tended by a herbalist, is probably what led to English flowerbeds. A walled garden was a secret place of contemplation, tranquillity and delicate blossoms, a cage for a princess, a stage where wan ladies could be surprised and wooed, or where they could just linger and wait. It's really the Arabs who gave gardens their abiding metaphor.

Their word was paradise; heaven was a garden. They took it to Spain and sour, thuggish Crusaders brought it back to England along with rose roots and lemons.

Chivalry developed a new complex allegory of flowers, and gardens grew courtly. But what really kicked gardening off for the English was the Dutch. It was William of Orange who brought the great Low Country bourgeois obsession with husbandry and bulbs to England and made it properly national in the sense that, from a cottage garden to a ducal park, everyone could join in with the national philosophy of vegetable triage. The garden was the perfect aesthetic for the Protestant English, who as a rule of green thumb distrusted and often despised the high arts and the hubristic construct of paint and marble. They didn't much care for books or music beyond a bawl and ugly dancing.

England has never been a nation in touch with its feminine side. It's never been able to express itself soberly or with delicacy, and it's made uncomfortable by those who do. The English mistrust art unless it's wrapped in a thick opaque layer of craft. They know how to appreciate the making; it's the hand, you see, not the head. So most of the great examples of English culture have been made by artists who refer to themselves as craftsmen, carpenters and builders, carvers, stitches and engravers. The garden came as a revelation to the English; it literally sprang from the Bible. To toil in the garden is neither art nor truly craft; it isn't strictly farming, it's in a category all on its own. If the Muslims saw the garden as a metaphor for heaven, so Protestant England could see it as the seed of Eden, the time of innocence and purity. The English garden is a profound and silent parable. In a garden you make without creating, you toil without payment; God is the creator, nature the maker. A gardener is simply the facilitator, the server, Nature's hod-carrier. All Englishmen believe that nothing man-made is as beautiful as a garden. This is almost the defining aesthetic difference between

Protestant England and Catholic Europe. All art, however grand or simple, has within it the vanity and the ego of the artist, but a garden is pure and incorrupt, a divine blessing, a psalm of nature.

Of course the English also understand that this is equivocal. The old joke has a new vicar passing a particularly verdant cottage garden. He says to the old gardener, 'Ah Fred, look at what glory the hand of God has wrought.' 'Oh yus, vicar, marvellous, but you should have seen it when he had it to his'self.' There is in the English garden a particular shade of melancholy, a remembrance of something lost; the concept of original sin is particularly vibrant in Protestantism. All gardens revisit the perfect place where sin was first born. It is also a perfect place for committing a few more. There's nothing conceived by the laws of God or man from serial murder to bestiality that the English won't joyfully transgress in a garden.

Nature has always been a raw metaphor for human and divine emotion, something that needs to be tamed for a finer and calmer purpose. So the English went about turning England from a secret forest into a new Eden. Primogeniture allowed land-owners to make parks, suitable for riding, hunting and flushing pheasants, whilst enclosing the common land into its now familiar cubist filigree of hedge and stone. That's the image Englishmen like to think of as their home. It became not so much the recreation of Eden as what Eden would have grown to look like if only God had had the foresight to exempt the English from expulsion. Every autumn dwindling congregations celebrate harvest festival. 'We plough the fields and scatter the good seed on the land, but it is fed and watered by God's almighty hand.' Jehovah patronized and reduced to a sort of gardener's apprentice. As the cornucopia of the goodness of the parish is laid along the aisle, punctuated with tins for those less fortunate, a visitor might receive the distinct sense that, rather than offering sacrifice on the altar for a bountiful God, the church is just showing him what he's been missing.

Whilst the watering can, secateurs, trowel and hoe are the instruments of English culture, so the garden was always supposed to be the great equalizer of society. There's an abiding piece of social mythology regularly exploited by PG Wodehouse, of the duke being mistaken for his gardener. All gardeners, whatever their status, must dress like peasants and spend a good deal of their time on their knees under the blue dome of nature's cathedral. Rain falls on duke and gardener's boy alike, and greenfly attacks the palace parterre and the tenement window-box.

You might have noticed that, although the English claim to be the font of all gardening wisdom, actually most of it came from other people. The great stately gardeners were by tradition all Scots; now they're Poles. England is a plagiarizing nation. As it spread out across the world, so the flora of the world came back. Its flowerbeds and rockeries boast plants from the Hindu Kush, the Yangtze Delta and the New Guinea Highlands. There's the monkey puzzle from Chile and the rhododendron from the Himalayas. The discovery of the new world almost doubled the available cultivars of the old. In the nineteenth century garden-ing became patriotic, the evocation of Empire. Indeed, one of the great and usually unremarked sagas of Empire was the transporta-tion of vegetables around the world to feed the workers of new industry, or as a cash crop. The *Bounty* was on its way to the South Seas to collect breadfruit for possible use as cheap food in the West Indies plantations of sugar-cane having been imported from Arabia. Cotton, tea, opium, maize, wheat and indigo were peddled round the world. English gardens became mini empires, so obviously stuffed with metaphors and similes and parables that they didn't really know where to begin. Life, death, time, vanity, patience, endurance, forthright purity and fecundity – there is hardly a quality or defect that couldn't be sermonized out of a garden. The language of the flowers themselves was as complex as a military code. Any emotion, every yearning or triumph, found embodiment in gardens.

It is odd that in the gardening section of any book shop there are yards and yards of volumes on the mechanics and aesthetics of plants, but very few exploring why you would want to garden. Or what a garden might mean. It's as if the English – that most literal of people – had simply all agreed not to mention the psychology, metaphysics, symbolism or Freudian truth of their national obsession. Look at their gardens and you will be as close as any outsider will ever get to seeing an audit of the English psyche. Look at them carefully and you'll notice that, from the grand rolling lawns of the country house to the repeated trenches of roses in the ribbons of suburban semis, there is never anyone in them. The last great mystery is that the English rarely venture into their gardens. Gardens, like churches, are for toiling in and not for loungeing in. There will be plenty of time to lie in them when you're dead.

The front gardens of London look particularly sumptuous this year. They're glossy with health and vigour; climbing things shin up drainpipes with Olympian ease, bushy things bustle and tall leggy things sway with a nonchalant elegance. Flowers open their faces with childlike exuberance, blossoms cling to precipitously humped-back boughs. Gardens reach out across the road, rolling dripping into the street, and trees ripple with muscular health. Green stuff is everywhere. Ferns squat in sunless basements, bedsit windowsills have bright boxes, stairs are clumsy with potted geraniums. The whole city is a poem, a prayer to the green man who has found his way through the tons of concrete and tarmac and the centuries of disbelief. He's sprouted through the cracks and blossomed.

It wasn't always like this. I can just remember the last pea-souper, where you couldn't see your hand in front of your face and the policemen wore masks, and the sulphurous coal-gas yellow air stole into the lungs of the old and carried them off by the tumbril-load. That was when London was still soot black and smelt of industrial fart, when the only things that would grow happily here were the London plane trees with their psoriasis-scaly bark; and variegated laurel, which needs neither light nor air nor water to eke out its miserly life; and privet, which poisons the earth around it. I was a gardener's mate once and had to grub up a London privet hedge. It was like a thing from a Nordic saga. It fought and clawed and coughed up dry dust and dead spiders with a manic ferocity. It had been part of the city before I was born. It had survived the weather, the neglect, the smog, the Depression and the Blitz and it wasn't coming out without a fight. I hacked and tugged and beat and dug and swore at it for a day, and it covered me in the filth of a century, wealed and flogged every inch of me, and I've hated privet ever since. And roses bloomed in London. Strange epicurean hypochondriac, exotic roses thrived in the fetid thick air and blossomed with a light frosting of soot. And that was it, except for the aspidistras that stood in front-room windows pressed against the grubby glass like naughty children, not allowed out to play.

But this has all changed. Today London looks as if it has been decorated by a naïve painter; it's a Gothic Ambridge on steroids and nitrate. The English can't see a perfect piece of architectural harmony and not think that it would be improved by a wisteria. I'm not entirely sure it's a good thing, this floral city. A city's primary defining characteristic is that it isn't the country. Yet in the city there is always a nostalgia for some muddy life that never was in bosky glades and florid lanes. The yearning for greenness is an abiding and essential component of urban life, half of which is made of wanting to be somewhere else, the other half a profound gratitude that you're not.

Perhaps the urge to grow things is a bit of a sentimental sigh, like a picture torn out of a magazine and stuck on the fridge. Some of the most glorious bits of countryside in England are in

cities, particularly in London, with its ravishing public parks –
slabs of greenery apparently held hostage by the bailey of tarmac
and motte of traffic. Parks and gardens aren't just memorials to
the country, buttonholes worn by towns, they are given purpose
and scale by the surrounding buildings.

The greatest celebration of a garden in this city is Chelsea
Flower Show, one of that handful of events that is the shorthand
summation of Englishness.

Chelsea is the biggest flower show in the world. The Trooping
the Colour, the Spithead Review of England's pre-eminence in
horticulture. But how absurd is it to hold an Olympics for
flowers, a competition where the competitors have no concept
of competing? To hand out medals and certificates to God or
nature. This is where the English vision of Eden, born in
monastery gardens and cottages, ended up. Only the English
could sneer at a plant for being common or gaudy. They practise
an extreme form of floral permorphism; the list of flowers that
are beyond the pale, below the salt, infra dig, is a who's who of
what's not.

The driving force of Chelsea is the subtle variegation and
shades of a veritable class system. Nature tamed and transformed
into an elaborate metaphor for snobbery. Chelsea is a familiar
English emulsion of staggering nastiness and winning dedication. But the nature and aesthetics of gardening is simply
horrible. Walking down Chelsea's tented avenues, past the
conservatories and gazebos countless to man, the ornamental
statuary, emetic fountains, garden seeds and *al fresco* dining-
tables, the plastic marble-effect tubs and distressed wrought-iron
planters, you can build up a forensic picture of a composite
people you'd gnaw though your own wrist to escape. The
abiding sense is of small-minded, suburban nostalgia seasoned
with aesthetically barren good taste.

Perhaps the most disturbing objects are the gaggles of naked
bronzite marbleish young girls who are on offer to stand, bend

and splay at the edge of ornamental water features or dribble down their pubescent nipples. They mimic the posers of classical sculpture with the pre-menstrual flexibility of ballet legs, straining to give tempting hints and glimpses of barely legal smudged vaginas. These children wait for some sweaty, knowing old hand to stroke their buttocks, fumble their breasts, press up behind them. They'll stand in patio-designed groups as if in a slave market. At their feet lie stone greyhounds and cement rabbits. The odour of repressed lust is shuddering.

Urban gardening is all repression and suppression. Gardening plainly means something very different to the English than it does to everyone else. It's a displacement activity, the expression of thwarted creativity, eroticism, distressing feelings of social insecurity and shapeless foggy violence. More than anything else, gardens are the burial grounds of the lumpy, throttling puce anger of the English. The vegetative eugenics practised in mild-mannered cul-de-sacs, the extreme prejudice of poisoning some blameless green thing while feeding another, are symptoms of a Pooterish yearning for a Fascist order.

Gardens are model train-sets of omnipotence hidden under the crazy paving and the ornamental windmills, and the best-laid patios are over first wives and random hitch-hikers. Burying bodies at the bottom of the garden is a very English concealment of crimes of neatness and embarrassment. This is a country that can force you to garden, where the parish or your neighbours can twist your arm, make you delve like Adam on behalf of the common neatness, like being made to join the party and take part in massacres. Best-kept village competitions turn stock-broker dormitory towns into little Stalingrads, where baskets of lobelia and geranium hang from lamp-posts in symbolic place of deserters and quislings.

12

Sport

When the winning city for the 2012 Olympics was announced, I was in east Greenland in a hotel room on the edge of the inhabited world with the 24-hour light on outside. I was flicking channels, and there was the German news. The scene cut from Trafalgar Square to the Place de la Concorde. The joy of London, the disappointment of Paris. What made it so vivid was that both cities were joined, for an instant, by exactly the same emotion – shock. Real jaw-dropping, hand-to-mouth shock. The French were beggared that they hadn't won, and the English were beggared that they had.

Looking out of the window, I could see the ice floes glowing mysteriously electric blue in the still Arctic. Little wooden houses painted happy colours with outside loos and no running water, and dog teams chained in the yard. They clung to the edge of the rocky shore like an invasion of Lego, and in the middle of town was an oblong, a flat piece of earth which had been graded and rolled with great care. It was the municipal football pitch. Flat land is at a premium in Greenland. They could have chosen to put any number of more civically useful things here, as there are only a couple of months each year when the pitch isn't frozen to iron or under six feet of snow, or blasted with winds that are twice as strong as hurricanes and could flay your face to the bone. But Eskimos love football. Teams come across the pack ice to play, and there were always kids on the pitch practising keepy-uppies, wearing Manchester United shirts over their thermal parkas, never having to come in when it gets dark.

After the language, football is England's greatest gift to the world. When all the other inventions are rust and junk, when the discoveries are commonplace, there will still be football. The only truly pan-national human activity, football is played on every continent; there isn't a child in the world who hasn't had a crack at goal. Football is the cliché of hope, an act of exuberance amongst hardship and squalor. Football, they tell us, is more than a game; it is a simple act that transcends language or borders – everybody speaks football. Setting up an impromptu game with local lads is one of the first passive things occupying armies do. Football matches are arranged as diplomacy and goodwill; they are also the fulcrums of animosity, violence and tribal pride.

Even saying these things about football is stating obvious truisms. We all know what football is and does. Even if we've never watched a game all the way through or followed a team, we know about South American referees who were shot for dodgy decisions and the players from the *favelas* and mud huts who made it to international stardom and riches. We all know the footballing parables.

I once saw a match in the Maracana Stadium in Rio de Janeiro, vast and brutally beautiful. God knows how many people it holds. This was where Brazil lost the World Cup to Uruguay and inconsolable Brazilians leapt from the roof. Brazil is the world's second team, and the Maracana is the beautiful game's Vatican. It's easy to start writing like that about football, and lots of people do. It's a cordoned-off area of junk writing at the back of every newspaper. Football isn't just a pan-international activity, it's a pan-international purple metaphor. As I sat in the stadium in Rio I wondered how a village yokels' rough-and-tumble game from muddy medieval England became an untiring, unvarying global soap opera and a philosophy. Why football? Why not skittles, or tug-of-war, or cheese-rolling? Football is a game of near-moronic simplicity and repetition. Whoever called it 'the beautiful game' must have been living in a cave with a burlap sack over their heads. The rules reduce down to 'don't use your hands', a self-imposed handicap. But there is within football a seed of inspired genius. It reaches some collective aspect of human nature, some hunter-acquisitive instinct.

I'm not much of a football fan, more of a fair-weather football father. I take my boy to see Chelsea occasionally and laugh in a disengaged way at the vicious humour of the terraces. I try to be an ironic observer, aware that this is a touchstone ritual of father-and-son-dom; but secretly, I'm also frightened of football. It's like standing on the edge of a precipice. I can feel its pull, sense its power. I know the true reason I keep my distance from this game; it's because if I allowed myself I could become as tunnel-visioned and enraptured by it as the millions and millions of poor indentured fans – week in, week out, round-the-world slaves to the results. Leisure life would be a *glissando* of air-punching triumph or knuckle-gnawing disappointment a jerky circle of emotion, a life-long tease of little false endings in a drama without a plot.

Investing that much emotion in a game that you have no control over, that you don't play in, that is run for sponsorship access to television and derivative clothing lines, that offers so much unproductive disappointment and triumph, is cultural suicide. But I can hear the siren call of the crowd and feel the prickle of addiction in the veins, that great primal sense of belonging, the salty comfort of shared misery. And it isn't only football.

The English have invented almost every game you can think of – and if they didn't invent them, they grabbed and codified them. Far too many games' rules have been constructed by the English for it to be merely coincidental. They have sat down and worked out all the possible variations of outcome, all the conceivable cheats and possible cul-de-sacs of children's play, and written the law for adults to play them, making them dry and serious. From polo to motor-racing, rugby to bridge, the English have been there to see that it's fair and, to coin one of their endless sporting truisms, that the playing-field is level. The English are the accountants and attorneys of fun. Fairness is an English thing – or rather unfairness is an English thing, a trigger for their rage. For the English, sport is the groyne that stands against anarchy, the pillar that prevents the triumph of bullying. Sport is the great changing-room of metaphor and simile.

The renaissance of sport in the nineteenth century served a practical purpose for a small country that had a lot of the world to administer. Games were a way of quickly and enjoyably working out leadership material, extolling and teaching all those things that the administrative class admired so much. Games, in particularly team games, fostered clannish bonding and homo-erotic hierarchy worship – all of which was held to be a good thing when dealing with lesser people. Games gave you a sense of honour and justice and were implicitly the gift and birthright of evolved societies. If you had to find a district commissioner, a magistrate, a police chief or a civil servant to run some lost corner of Empire, then a games captain or a boy with House Colours was as good a bet as any. The purpose of Empire was trade; it needed calm and consistency, and sport was a pretty good management training tool. The English had to work with the material to hand – there weren't that many Englishmen and there was an awful lot of Empire. Even the slowest and most ponderous public schoolboy could understand a set of rules if they came with a bat and ball.

The English work hard to foster a reputation for being scrupulously fair, along with being simple-minded and resolute. This concept of sport as a training wasn't invented by the English; like so much of their culture, it was borrowed from the classics. Games as civic duty were a Greek invention for training citizen soldiers and measuring heroes, without actually having to spill blood. Sport was inseparable from religion. Games were votive offerings, intrinsic parts of religious festivals, and the English liked the muddy allusion for their practical, simply and earthy religion. They were comfortable with the parable of selfless sporting achievement as being the imitation of divinity and simultaneously a model for business. Games neatly bridged God and Mammon.

The English added something else, a basket of sporting metaphors that the Greeks and the Romans had never considered – and no other nation has been able to stomach. For the English, real character is built not by winners, but by losers. Anyone can be a good winner. Winning is a spiritually calorific but essentially unnourishing experience. It grows fat ego and invites flabby hubris. It is in losing that the individual really discovers what they're made of, and it was in coming a good second that the kernel of the truth in the lesson of sport lay, because winning a game of muddied oafs or flannelled fools is transiently unimportant, but being able to cope with failure and disappointment, to turn around the headlong impetus of adrenalin, effort, expectation and hope, and still shake hands with your opponent and pick up the bat or the boot the next day – that's the proving and honing and the toughening of character.

The English don't like winners, and they don't like people who behave like winners. The best thing to do if you're caught winning is to slip away blushing. If you're cornered, then mutter something about luck and flukes. Losing is what the English are comfortable with, they understand its value. They pick at their 1966 World Cup triumph like a scab that won't heal. I actually watched it in gritty black and white on our tiny television. I remember the utterly unbearable intensity of the expectation, the cruelty of the growing possibility that the English might win, the agony, and then the final whistle and the uncomfortable, awful English truth that the nation would have to live with this aberration, this atypical blot. It was that childhood branding shock that convinced me I should do everything to avoid being a sports fan of any sort.

The American ideal that winning is everything, that there is first and then there is nowhere, that only triumph rates, builds rather feeble characters who are easily dashed. The game was never the point, the point was how you played it. That's what the rules were for. All this is still an incomprehensible tautology to much of the world, but it has been an incomparable boon to the collective power of the English. They have learnt that the long game is not measured in how well or how often you win, but in the quality of your defeat.

My favourite sporting event is the palio, a horse race that is run twice a year in Siena. As the English wrote the rule book for sports, there is a certain sameness to them all, a bland English wholesome goodness, a studied rather humourless seriousness about the atmosphere of sport. The palio is proof that there are other models, that sport doesn't have to be based on scrupulous fairness, justice and transparency. The palio is a marvellous lasagne of duplicity, cheating and sharp practice that has been built into the race over hundreds of years. Horses are drugged, jockeys are bribed, secret alliances are made and double-crosses are frequent. No aspect of possible underhand advantage is overlooked. The race can only begin when the tenth and last horse in the line has been sufficiently bribed to start running. This can take hours. The race itself is over in a bone-hectic glorious ninety seconds, but the sport of it has been played out for weeks. Millions of euros are spent on the palio, and the city of Siena devotes a ridiculous and marvellous portion of its energy to staging it.

Winning and losing are the biggest things in the *contradas'* lives and when they do lose, they don't call foul or say it was unfair, they say, 'We didn't cheat well enough. We didn't bribe efficiently.' The palio is a looking-glass glimpse at what all sport might have been if the Renaissance city states had got hold of the rule books ahead of the English.

It has always rather galled the English that the modern Olympiad was the invention of the French. But, being practised good losers, they would never say so. The French saw something else in sport; when the English wanted character-building, the French saw diplomacy by other means. The classical Olympics were truces between warring states, and they were a model for the spirit of fraternity and equality that the French like to think is their particular forte. The Olympics were to be an extension of the enlightened global socialism of the French revolution. When I got back to London a week after the announcement that London had won the bid, no one mentioned the Olympics, it had become rather embarrassing. England has a few years to turn it into a heroic failure, to pray for bad weather. And all over the country small children were purposefully putting on their trainers to embark on a long and gruelling road driven by a dream – to become plucky little losers in front of a quietly appreciative home crowd.

13

Political Correctness

The first recorded use of the phrase 'politically correct' was in 1793. A.J. Wilson said in the Supreme Court that, 'the United States, rather than the people of the United States is the toast given and this is not politically correct.' Who was doing the toasting we're not told, and it's not really relevant. This disembodied free-floating sentence drips down to us from 200 years ago. A shard of overheard chat, a dry moment in a dull monologue.

Mr Wilson couldn't possibly have known that this is what he'd be remembered for, though not many of us do remember him even for that. But he's there in the reference books, bracketed and italicized and all hung about with the little abbreviations of lexicography. Old Mr Wilson – for some reason I assume he was old – couldn't possibly have known of the fury that would be made of this conjunction of words. Each smooth and featureless. Of course, his was not the use we associate with political correctness, but it is out there, and it has a prophetic tone. In the chaos of recorded thought, this is the stroke of the butterfly wings that eventually grows into the hurricane.

The first use of political correctness in the sense that we all understand it is by a T. Cade, who wrote in a book called *Black Woman*, 'A man cannot be politically correct and a chauvinist too.' That was in 1972. And since then we've had thirty-odd years of variously intense forms of political correctness. A generation of English men and woman have grown up in a country that has been exercising withering scorn and splenetic fury at new words and new meanings through old words.

We're now used to hearing talk of ethnic minorities and black people, of the developing world and gays. We no longer think of these things as being particularly politically correct; they are simply names for people, places and things. If you look up 'political correctness' on the web, you'll find nearly two million entries. As far as I can be bothered to tell, every single one of them is against it. Political correctness is a mass crime, a polite holocaust that hurt no one and has no perpetrator. It is a global movement that's changed the language of politics and society in a more profound way than anything since the King James Bible.

Political correctness has no author, no statesman, no elected representatives, no theorists, no demagogues, and it has absolutely no popular backing. No one will stand up and say, 'Yes, I'm politically correct'; everybody is against it, thinks it appalling, embarrassing, stupid, irritating, prissy and mealy-mouthed. Political correctness is the Scarlet Pimpernel of social engineering. Newspapers and magazines run regular, sniggering little columns pointing out new outbreaks of PC: clumsy sentences, lines in council guidelines or instructions for shop assistants, public notices and teachers' notes. It's as if some language liberator had stolen past in the night, substituting 'disabled' for 'handicapped' and stealing the 'man' from 'chairman', replacing an Eskimo with an Inuit and swapping the 'dustman' for a 'refuse collector'. No one is ever caught red-taped, or publicly pilloried for the nicey-nicing of the language, but the web is full of conspiracies as to the origins of PC. My favourite is the absolutely po-faced, so-historical treatise explaining that it was a movement of European socialists to undermine the idea of the individual as the holder of singular and inalienable thought, by subtly altering the language and thereby removing our ability to think sensibly and assertively. We will then be a pushover for the westward colonization of communists, where the collective will is everything and the individual of no consequence. There is another, similar screed exposing PC as a Roman Catholic plot for much the same sort of reasons and ends.

PC's rationale is that general terms have specific individual consequences, that people have the right to a say in how they're known and that, whilst respect is something that individuals have to earn, it's also something that groups and sections of society have a reasonable right to expect. Like many conspiracy theories, after you've stripped away the paranoia there is a fanciful truth. In this case it's the belief that you can engineer ideas with language – change the word and you alter the thought.

As there is no one else who will stand up and offer two cheers for political correctness, let me do it. I can't claim to have invented political correctness or sat in on the secret cabal that drew up the hit-list of dubious terms. I can't even say that I work hard to remove 'nigger brown' from haberdashers' colour charts or make all thespians equal as 'actors' regardless of gender. In fact, I have often been called politically incorrect as a compliment. I regularly get letters from people who assume that I will share their disgust at not being able to call a spade a coon any more in a general, non-specific, non-judgemental, jokey sort of way, and I've been taken to the Race Relations quango by the Welsh. The case was dismissed (apparently the Welsh are beyond insult).

But political correctness is a good thing. It has changed the vernacular of politics and society. The modest truth about PC is that its aims are so modest, so uncontentious. How could you possibly find fault with wanting to put people at their ease – being polite and not offering unintended offence? If you put that in an opinion poll, who would say no? It's such an obvious and innocuous accommodation. It costs nothing more than the thought to change a word here and there, and the result is equally small but important. A term of address, an added politeness, doesn't get anyone a job or a better house or an education or a free lunch, but it does indicate that the user is aware of those other things and that you want them to be better. That you want those whom you address and talk about to be part of a pluralistic, accommodating, comfortable society. This is such a truism that it's embarrassing to have to reiterate it. In fact, it is the live and let live, fair play, don't disturb the horses thing that the English like to think of as their invention and birthright.

But the free and great benefits of political correctness collide with another self-defining Englishman's thing. The right – nay, the obligation – to speak as you find. To talk straight. Not to mince words. To be awkward and honest. PC is a small curb on the right of the English to say any word in their language whenever the mood takes them. To graze unfettered across the dictionary without being fenced or told that they must stick to the footpath, or keep off the adjectives. Political correctness is thought to be the most popular and expertly used prop of English confrontation, the thin end of the wedge.

PC wants to confiscate words. It wants to censor – to offer, low-fat, high-fibre, committee words instead of steak and kidney English, and the English won't have it. In truth and practice, PC does exactly the opposite. It adds more words and alternative words to the language. It makes the tongue richer, stronger, more nimble and delicate. No one can corral a word or wilfully make it extinct. What the thin end of the wedge did was to prop open the door and free up old words from their sticky, offensive meanings and give them back to the people to whom they belonged. So 'nigger, queer and paki' became labels that niggers, queers and pakis could use themselves as they saw fit. That seems to me not to be a limiting of language, but an imaginative freeing of it.

Neither does it mean that they are any less offensive or loaded with venom when fired with intent. What the middle-brow speakers of middle English really hate is the whiff, the hint, the gossamer veil of euphemism. Euphemism is the varnish on the thick end of their wedge and they hate it. The devil is in euphemism. It qualifies and mocks plain talk. PC could have been called euphegenics or euphemismics or euphemera and again the joke is that the fruit and the flower of the English language is the lushness and the verdant depths, the heady scent and the vibrating hues of its euphemisms. The spinneys of simile, coppices of allegory and the Elysian hardwood forest of metaphor.

English is so far and away the most successful language that hurdled teeth, because it has more ways of saying more things than any other language. Not just a few more ways, but an A-Z, a directory of other ways. Political correctness is a particularly Anglophone concern, principally because so many other languages don't have the luxury of choice. To complain that the substitution of some words is the beginning of a monosyllabic famine is like complaining that anyone who fills an egg cup with sea water is going to empty the ocean. What political correctness really is, is etiquette. The man-made rules, whose initial and principal purpose is the smooth and equitable running of society.

Tom Paine, the English revolutionary of American freedom, said: 'Manners are the highest achievement of a civic culture.' A society without etiquette is not a society, it's a mob. No, even mobs have rules. Manners work without legislation or police force, without prisons or fines or the intervention of the state. Yet they have stewarded our lives and the lives of every group of humans since we learnt to stand upright. Etiquette is older than spoken language, and PC has tapped into this prehistoric network of understanding to make a small correction in order to smooth out a few of the little unfairnesses of living in a huge, unequal and complicated society. It has, in a generation, made us recognize our responsibility to everyone else, and in particular those who suffer the most from being marginalized, and those who have a history of being abused and exploited.

It's been done in the teeth of huge odium and fury, and that has been a strange corollary benefit of political correctness. It's a padded cell for the free-floating anger that is the hallmark of the English – so many fierce little letters to the papers, so many sneered rants at dinner tables and smart, caustic jokes. There has been no let-up in the flecked loathing that spat at political correctness, but the anger has done precious little to wipe the soft smile off the PC face, or prevent the euphemistic housekeeping. The anger is funnelled into a cul-de-sac of letters and jokes and obsessive collections of numpties who set up committees for plain-speaking and old-fashioned English, who write little books of gruff, grammatical rudeness. There is no one to blame, no one to throw an egg at or assassinate, no one to vote out. PC is a great, soft, anger-management cushion. It absorbs the head-butts, the kicks and the jabs of the intellectually yobbish, the thuggery that lurks in the third bottle of a dinner party.

The violent objection to political correctness is the engine that keeps it rolling. If no one cared one way or the other, then PC would have expired in a puddle of good intentions and unconcern, but the anger that motivates the name-calling itself begets name-changing. Political correctness has a symbiotic relationship with the thing it tries to change, it is an amazing construct, a piece of public etiquette that attracts and absorbs and diffuses the dismal bigotry it's designed to change; and by so doing gains strength. It is a placebo and a cure and a fire that's made hotter by having cold water poured over it; it is a peculiarly English-speaking push-me-pull-you.

Despite the collective English belief that the language is inimitable and totemic and the granite spine of the nation, and that it sits in judgement on our grammar and our syntax like a fierce-bearded Victorian headmaster with a quill to correct apostrophes in one hand and a cane for split infinitives in the other. In fact, language isn't like that at all. It's a fairground. All flashing lights and shrieks and exclamations. It's a giggly debutante who can't decide which word to use. It's fashionable, forgetful, imported patois. Very few things in England are quite as suggestible, quite such a pushover as its language. It is a magpie that picks up slang and pecks apart convention with a wilful abandon.

Whenever the language behaves like an infuriating, mumbling adolescent, it is at its most brilliant. It's there that it will produce poetry and drama and songs and pyrotechnic expressions. English is as new as the most recent refugee, it's a brilliant, invisible river that flows all round us, full of things that we've left unsaid. It is deeper than you will ever manage to plumb and faster than you will ever patter. This voice is the greatest gift and blessing of the English, a language that is the defining quality of its humanity and the pinnacle of its culture.

14

Queues

Queues, like roundabouts, are one of those things that have come to symbolize the Englishness of the English. The queue is a parable and a prescription. For the English the queue is more important than just fair and predictable play; it's self-medication against the family madness. It is also a brilliantly simple idea. Typically English in the sense that it's the distillation of complicated and sophisticated ethical, political and social considerations. The English are particularly good at and fond of shaping complex ideas and issues into easy-listening aphorisms. And the queue is one of their best – it's wholly democratic and classless, it's not predicated on cash, looks, brains or muscle. It's so straightforward that even cattle understand it. The queue is properly anarchic – anarchy being not a free-for-all in the sense of competing selfishness, but a free-for-all in the sense of collective responsibility; and when you look at it like that it seems so wholly un-English. A place where the Duke stands behind the butler and the Dame behind the lap-dancer – all organized without the need of a big stick. There is no common law pertaining to queues, no high-court judgement. Queues weren't mentioned in the Magna Carta or the Book of Common Prayer; there's no nursery rhyme game about queuing. The queue involves no equipment – it is a perfect piece of organic social engineering.

So how did the English ever come by it and agree to stand in it without demur or complaint and wait their turn in the Dunkirk spirit, that taciturn ability to outlast adversity? The photographs of those lines of soldiers on the French beaches, snaking up to their armpits in cold water, exhausted and frightened and beaten, queuing to get onto destroyers and little pleasure launches, are a cliché of Englishness. They evoke the image the English like to see reflected in their shaving mirrors.

Dunkirk was the lowest ebb of English fortune since the Norman Conquest, and the men survived by the skin of their teeth because of a queue. If there'd been a continental free-for-all at Dunkirk, if everyone had rushed and shoved and barged, the miracle wouldn't have happened – the Army would never have made it back to the south coast. The European war would probably have been lost and that would have been that. Or at least the start of a very different story. You could say in a simple English sort of way that the war was won – or at least not lost – because of a queue. So the queue has a particular place in the English pantheon.

The queue is now mostly noticed by its absence. It has become yet another grimly spit-polished plaque in the mausoleum of nostalgia, along with hat-doffing and chips in newspaper and clips around the ear. Bus stops are now gaggles rather than neat lines; tubes and trains are a clamour of elbows. But they still seem to work. We all get on in much the same order that we waited.

Queues don't start, they form like stalactites or clouds. Queues are an act of God or nature for the English, who do them quite naturally – up to tills in chemists, at cinemas, at weddings and funerals and, I'm told, in brothels. It's not that they do it uncomplainingly; they don't complain about queuing, but they do complain in queues about everything else. Indeed the social currency of a queue is complaint. The queue is a small, disposable culture all of its own; membership is like belonging to a club with an infinite potential number of members. Being the member of a queue counts as an introduction, so the English will talk to each other in queues where they wouldn't dream of muttering a word to each other in church. But why did the English start queuing?

The word itself is originally from the old French – it's a heraldic term for the tail of a beast, and it referred to a Chinaman's pigtail for a hundred years before it came to its present meaning quite late in the nineteenth century. It's a word that must have grown from that great makeover the English did on themselves as a result of industry and Empire and missionary Christianity. It's a word for a newly dense population of mechanization, factories, tenements, crowded streets and traffic jams; of soup kitchens and charity – a word above all of order and control. Self-control.

Every English person has a cautionary tale, an apocryphal story, about those who transgress the un-law of queues – often foreigners. I've just been told this one, a story of a ski-lift. Apparently the lift was a little funicular. It pulled into a platform, its doors opening and closing automatically. People hopped on, clipping their skis to a rack on the side. The queue was long. As my storyteller got to the platform a band of strapping Germans loudly shoved their way to the front and jumped into the next empty car. The rest of the queue looked on in fury, the automatic doors closed and the Germans stared back with their characteristic mien of Germanic entitlement and triumphalism. 'We came to ski, not to stand in line,' their faces said. And then just as the car began to move, a slight middle-aged man, an Englishman of no distinction with a look of calm determination, trotted onto the platform and unclipped the German skis, laying them with exaggerated care on the platform. German faces were wiped with impotent indignation and mimed threats. The queue erupted into polyglot cheers, the little Englishman was slapped on the back. His hand was wrung and he made his way back to his place in the queue.

Now, the Englishman who told me this story said that

nothing that had ever happened to him had made him as incandescently angry as the German queue-bargers – or as elated as the revenge of the little man. It had filled him with such a cosmic release of transcendent happiness and pride in the chap's very ordinariness, that it had taken all his blightily prep-school-taught discipline not to burst into tears. 'It still pricks my eyes when I think of it, and you know the really important bit, he went back to his place in the queue. No one would have gainsaid his right to jump into the next carriage, he'd earned it. But the queue was more important than one man. You should have seen him, he'd have been played by John Mills in the film.'

This story, pathetic and embarrassing as it is, fulfils all the criteria for a British war movie. The baddies are of course German and, pushed beyond the constraints of a natural reticence and shyness, the little Englishman takes on the muscled might of the Krauts with pluck, derring-do and guile, saving Europe before blushingly returning to his allotted position in life.

The storyteller's response is hardly rational. A few people getting ahead of you makes little difference to your day, it isn't going to dent your allotted span. But the queue isn't about outcomes or destination, it's about the journey and the manner in which you make it. A queue is like life. It's an allegory of English life. To transgress against the queue is a sin against the English, and they can become draconian in its defence.

Draco, by the way, was an Athenian who in 621 BC was given the task of modernizing the law. He attempted to take personal vengeance out of justice so that all crimes – with the exception of murder – would be against the state, not the victim. Consequently the punishments were notoriously eye-watering, even by pre-Christian standards.

I'm surprised that more English children aren't called Draco – he is a very English man in the way that utter foreigners, such as Prince Philip, can be. The queue stands for the right of every

English person and the retribution – the fury – it can ignite isn't personal, it's on behalf of the nation. The English talk a lot about fairness, mostly in its perceived absence and the *un*fairness of things. In most areas of life fairness is blurred, murky and diluted, but a queue is pristine and perfect. It is absolute, right and wrong. To join the end is fair, to try and get in at the beginning is unfair. Feel the frisson behind you in a queue if a friend joins you – it is only just allowable and everyone will have ascertained your exact relationship. The anger that the queue empowers is righteous, and how often in a month of Sundays do we get permission to vent righteous anger as opposed to the common-or-garden self-interested kind?

Never undervalue the pleasure an Englishman can extract from being both right and angry simultaneously. If you ever find yourself on the sticky end of an Englishman with a righteous grievance and you want to wound him mortally, capitulate instantly and apologize profusely – you will see a look of agonized consternation on his face, a childlike disappointment. You have taken away the bone he was so looking forward to picking. I did it in a hotel once. I checked in ahead of a middle-aged couple who'd had a bad flight and, finding themselves abroad, were girding themselves for ten days of unremitting grumble and complaint. They couldn't believe their luck when, not paying attention, I barged to the front of their two-person queue.

Discovering that I was also from home was added sand in their factor 30. A foreigner would have shrugged and rolled his eyes, but I would have to take it like an Englishman – except that I'm not, and I wasn't about to. I know these people. I know where this leads. So I said sorry, abjectly, and I smiled beatifically. Now, if there's one thing an Englishman can't abide it's an apology before he's finished. Combined with a smile, it's akin to sodomy without an introduction.

For a few seconds the Englishman closed his eyes, trying to

pretend he hadn't heard, but his biblical righteousness was running away, his plug was pulled. He followed me like a puffing, bulgey-eyed pug and said, finally: 'You can't just say sorry. You can't just say sorry, you know. I demand . . . I demand an apology.' Only an Englishman could have said that, and only someone who'd lived with the English could understand that it wasn't a tautology or a contradiction.

The English queue because they have to. If they didn't they'd kill each other. The pressure of boiling anger in the average post office is only contained by the shared knowledge that this is as fair as can possibly be arranged in this life. They would rip the head off Mahatma Gandhi if he tried to renew his TV licence ahead of them. The English queue where the rest of the world barges because the English need to queue. It's the tail of the mythic beast; tails add balance and equilibrium.

It's the young who are blamed for the decline in queuing discipline. They're accused of lacking the moral fibre, the civic responsibility and the diligence to stand in single file. It's not true. The young join far more queues than their parents ever did. To a disinterested observer, queuing is what the young do most. When anxious mothers lie sleepless in bed imagining their children injecting heroin into their eyeballs in squats beyond the railway line, or driving stolen Allegros the wrong way round ring-roads, fearless on Ecstasy and alcopops – actually the truth is much more likely to be that they're quietly queuing to get into a minute sweat-slick basement underneath Debenhams.

Drive around Soho or Brixton, Notting Hill or Hoxton after midnight, and what you'll see are remarkably docile queues of youngsters waiting to be let into clubs. This generation probably spends more of its time in suspended expectation than any since the days of rationing. But with the perversity and contrariness that is the trademark of rebellious youth, they've contrived to keep all that is boring and tiresome about queues and surrender the point of the exercise. Children queue for nightlife in the dark in the cold and the rain for hours, wasting their expensive homework- and worry-eroded leisure time, and when they do finally get to the head of the queue some clipboard Anubis says 'no' because they've got the wrong sort of hair or shoes or trousers or just look like kids.

On a whim the true egalitarian nature of the queue has been lost. Famous, notorious, beautiful, rich, exotic people are given carte blanche to bypass the queue altogether. This is expected. And indeed seems to add to the lure of the queue. Why would you take a thing of such simple, efficient, fair beauty and mutate it into humiliation and indefensible unfairness? The answer must in part be in the uncomfortable cocktail of youth, optimism and insecurity. If they think they will all be let in, then what would be the point of queuing for a club that would let just anyone in simply because they waited in line? The rejection on grounds of looks, trendiness, fame and caprice is what gives a club its cachet – being rejected only confirms that you were in the right place to begin with. You might have been the wrong person, but it was the right place.

Why don't kids rise up like the *sans culottes*, shout equality, fraternity and liberality and storm these little dungeon bastilles of unfairness and caste? Fairness is, after all, what children profess to care about, and they're naturally prone to take kicking, spitting umbrage at any minutely perceived insult. But it's the queue itself that seems to act as a restraint, that exerts a cool collective social pressure to conform and behave. Even though its purpose has been cynically manipulated, it still maintains order.

Airports are the maternity units of queues. Queue factories. Squirming orgies of queues. You could look at an airport and assume that its main purpose is the maintenance and invention of queues. Flying and travelling are simply by-products. Queues have to end somewhere. They have to do something.

There must be thousands and thousands of queues at Heath-
row, every hour curling and shuffling, petering out and reforming, merging and dispersing. There are queues in the
terminals, outside in the slip-roads, down along the motorways
and up high above us, turning like polite vultures in the damp
air. There are queues in computers and on telephones, queues of
trolleys and of luggage. I reckon that each traveller in an airport
queues at least six times. You are now asked to set aside two
hours for queuing. The reasons for a queue – checking in,
passport control, X-rays – are all quite swift and rudimentary.
Whatever their supposed importance, they seem anti-climactic,
merely a repetitive motion, but each is slightly different and the
taste and feel of the queues that lead up to them vary subtly. The
intensity of anxiety changes pitch; the worry and expectation
are all mixed to make a few hours in an airport a comprehensive
emotional colour chart.

The real point of the queue is the queuing. You can see in an
airport that a queue becomes a collective identity. They are
simply organisms with their own rules and aims and genetic
imperative to repeat themselves, to breed smaller queues that
will in turn become large queues, fade and die, sending out their
individual spore for yet more young queues. There's a natural life
cycle here, an ecology of lines separate but related, omnisexual.
Queues have a robust internal mechanism, an instinct to protect
themselves, to find their space, to curl and fold, stretch and
colonize. They are opportunistic. Benign and parasitic. The
perfect queue would of course be a circle, growing and shuffling,
moaning and sighing to itself, everyone the head and the tail,
both first and last. This may be an English image of heaven.

The one queue where the English revert to their natural shirty,
furious, awkward, murderous selves is the electronic one. Those
metallic voices that tell you you're held in a queue and that the
operator will get to you as soon as possible and that, by the way,
your call is very important, inspire the English to ruddy,

apoplectic, nose-severing wrath. Somehow queues don't work if they're virtual. You cannot queue on your own, you need to be in the company of others who are the same as you. They have to be tangible, we need to sense their encouragement and strength and the cold comfort of the line. We won't be fooled by a mechanical voice or an operator in Hyderabad.

The social ability to queue is a prerequisite for travelling. You have to be able to put aside your immediate hurry for the common good. In the countries that haven't as yet evolved the queue, getting anywhere is a nightmare of stasis and wasteful impotent confusion. Airports in Third World countries can be the departure of the fittest, usually exceedingly fat women with attached infant. One of the small pleasures of returning to England from abroad is the order and exaggerated politeness of the baggage carousel; even after a twelve-hour flight folded in half, the English see the queue of the bags as a tattoo of nationalism. You can instantly tell the foreigners; there is an eye-catching brow-raising hint of tough national pride and a sub-audible word to the wise for Johnnie Foreigner – you're in England now, that's not how we behave. We queue. We stand behind the line. You stand behind me.

An Englishman's life is measured in queues. He queues to be born, for dinner, for school, at college. He queues to shake hands with the bride and groom, queues for a house, queues for benefits, at the supermarket, at the bar, at the cashpoint, for a donor. He queues for the bathroom, for the football and the concert. He queues to pass the Cenotaph to pay his respects, take Communion, walk through the lobby, join a golf club, get to work, get home. He queues for a hip, a heart, a hope, a pension – and he queues at the crematorium. I find all that contrarily comforting. The queue insists that we travel at the pace of the weakest and the slowest, that no one gets left behind. That we all get to the further shore together or not at all. We are all queuing up to our armpits in cold water.

15

Letchworth Garden City

My first clumsy stab at a grand romantic gesture, an act clutched from too much Malory and Guinness, happened at the end of the summer term in 1969. I must have been just sixteen. I hurdled stealthily through the pre-dawn semi-detached front gardens of Letchworth Garden City pulling the heads off roses and shoving the petals down the front of my jersey.

When I had a sufficiently impressive floral paunch, I jogged back through the empty, neat streets, crept up to the girls' forbidden dormitory and dumped the lot – strew is, I expect, the word I'd have used – on Polly's bed. They were cold and damp with dew and live with greenfly. Polly was surprisingly gracious about being treated like compost, or a Hindu funeral pyre. Though impressed, touched and moved in a metaphysical sense, she whispered that she had double physics first thing and hadn't done her geography prep, so all things considered she'd rather go back to sleep for a couple of hours than indulge me in pressing, touching and moving in the earthly physical sense.

It's never a good moment to go back to school – reversing time's flywheel stirs up more than it settles. The platform at King's Cross was horribly familiar; the little rolling commuter train dumped me forty minutes later at Letchworth Station. With a sudden panic I thought I probably wouldn't remember how to find my way; I couldn't picture the town at all, couldn't place a single street, and then I walked out through the station concourse and it rose up in front of me like a solid tidal wave of memory. Every step and lane and cul-de-sac as precise as engraving. I had been prepared for it all to look smaller, meaner, less important, but I hadn't been prepared to feel twelve again. That dull, low-grade despair of going back to school and the cud bitter loathing of this town. Oh how we despised Letchworth, mocked and sneered at its inhabitants.

It's in the nature of English public schools to look down on the towns that give them space. It's an irony from the brimming English irony bucket. They all claim to be moulding decent upright young men and women to be *über*-servants of the community, but they can't even get them to buy a Mars Bar next door without braying abuse and getting into fights.

Letchworth has just celebrated its centenary – hence the rose. Nobody outside Letchworth noticed much, there was no national recognition, the Queen didn't pay a visit, the Prime Minister didn't make a speech, there was no service of thanksgiving, no three-part documentary, though there *was* an edition of *Songs of Praise*. In the English fashion of fetishizing what is wrong and ignoring what is right, Letchworth, the first Garden City, was ignored. But it was one of the most important and influential places ever built – as inspired as Wren and Hooke's plans for post-inferno London or Haussmann's Paris, as revolutionary as Niemeyer's Brasilia, more practical and longer lasting than a Frank Lloyd Wright millionaire's weekend home. Letchworth was conceived and made by a man who, if there were any sense of place and precedent in England, would have a statue in Trafalgar Square and his face on a bank note.

Ebenezer Howard is not a name the English conjure with. He wasn't built in their mould of heroism, he didn't swash the Empire or buckle the French; he wasn't vain, he didn't turn a phrase or thump a tub; he wasn't glorious or loud, or prematurely defunct. He wasn't an architect, an engineer, an empire-builder, a plutocrat or an industrialist, inventor or discoverer. His only practical aptitude was typing, and for most of his working life he was a shorthand stenographer in the House of Commons. A man whom even his admirer George Bernard Shaw could only manage to call 'an elderly nobody'. But he was a revolutionary, and a very English one. He was the home-grown antidote to his contemporary Karl Marx.

Howard didn't just imagine some idyllitarian Jerusalem, he actually built it in the green and pleasant land. His was a revolution so complete, so pervasive, that it radically and permanently affected not only the way the English lived, but how people live around the world. He dreamt and made the dream brick. What he invented were the suburbs – the way most of us live today – and it all began with Letchworth.

England in the 1880s and '90s was a nation seething with discomfort. The land was full of -isms and factions. In every back room and cellar, in every pub, there were wild-eyed Utopians pressing for something new, something radical – usually something either violent or made by artisans in smocks with a neo-gothic motif. It was a Tolkienesque menagerie of reformers: William Morris, the Fabians, Ruskin, George Bernard Shaw, H. G. Wells, John Stuart Mill, Herbert Spencer, Marx and Engels and the anarchist Prince Kropotkin. There were chartists, anarcho-syndicalists and the dissenting chapels. There were the unions and ferocious intellectuals and awkward self-taught agitator refugees, carrying the brooms, picks and scythes of communes, rebellions and coups that had blown across Europe, where constitutions were being rewritten, borders redrawn, royalty and the ancient order uprooted. New shirts and hats, new salutes and a new class of European were itchy with change. It seemed only a matter of time before Britain would pupate into something new and modern. Something European. Everyone had a plan and a grievance.

Dissent is an English speciality. How the nation managed to avoid spring-cleaning the old order at the end of the nineteenth century is one of the great strokes of luck or missed opportunities of English history. It's as if, knowing their true nature, they pulled back, and having been at this crossroads before, seeing where the road led, the English sub-consciously and collectively paused, understanding that once the radical hare had been set running, the dogs of discontent and reform would slip out of control.

In many ways England had more reason than most of its neighbours to want to divest itself of the old and invest in the new. It might be that the very cacophony of conflicting ideas and plans, the deluge of pamphlets, actually diffused the revolution into a series of damp squibs and half-cocked despair. Why Ebenezer Howard should have emerged as something of a hero out of this soup is a mystery; nobody knows why he became interested in land reform and improved housing. Perhaps it was whilst doing his job, recording the wind and bombast of the Commons. More likely it was because he'd lived for a time in Chicago and seen the new city rising at neck-wrenching speed.

As a young man he tried being a farmer on the great prairies, apparently without much success. In 1898, however, he published a short book called *Tomorrow: a peaceful path to real reform.* As a revolutionary tract it's short on rousing sentiment and purple prose. It even lacks a snappy title. It didn't call for the blood of martyrs or the sweat of labouring hordes; it's a rather dull and pedestrian guide book, an instruction manual to a place that didn't exist, with suggestions on how to build a future. Howard realized that the answer to social unrest and inequality wasn't firing squads and new constitutions written in gore and ashes, but better air, more space and decent housing. It was a studiedly parochial answer to the great pan-European anger of the nineteenth century. He pointedly opened the book with a quote from a now mostly unread American poet, James Russell Lowell: 'Nor attempt the future's portal with the past's blood-rusted key.' What Howard proposed was the *third way* of living (and if that sounds familiar, he got there first). Not industrial metropolis or agrarian cottage, but somewhere in between, somewhere that utilized the best of both.

The great cities of the late industrial revolution and high Empire were filthy, squalid places. The life expectancy in Liverpool, Manchester, Sheffield, Glasgow or the greatest city on earth, London, was falling. The huge profits made by industry and trade had created lives for industrial workers that were actually getting worse. Their living conditions were a sordid sin. The diseases and deformities of industry were a staggering lexicon of neglect, both ancient and modern. Even as late as 1914, one in ten volunteers for the Army was thought unfit for duty – this for a war that would use up bodies with an industrialized, cannibalistic greed, and even invented special regiments for stunted soldiers.

And rural England wasn't much better. The 1880s and '90s saw a severe agricultural depression. Indeed most of the nineteenth century, from the end of the Napoleonic wars, had been catastrophic for the rural economy. Farmers suffered from the opening-up of America and Australian arable production. The purpose of Empire was to make markets for British manufacturing, but the goods had to be paid for with something, and as often as not it was agriculture. By the last decade of the century cereal production in England was down by a quarter; living conditions for agricultural labourers were as bad, if not worse, than their industrial cousins; wages were pitiful and work often fitful. The infrastructure of old estates and tied cottages was neglected to decrepitude.

Altogether, the maintenance of green England was in a parlous state. Howard's third way was to make a human-sized town of detached houses with gardens, with its own schools and hospital, and rail and road links sustained by its own light industry. The citizens of the new Garden City would be part modern industrial worker and part agricultural smallholder. The gardens would grow fruit and vegetables, the workers would be able to walk to a clean factory, the town was to be surrounded by countryside, a green belt as it was newly minted, an idea first suggested by Colonel William Light, who designed Adelaide.

The building of the new cities of Empire, as well as the disgusting state of the old cities of home, were what inspired the Garden City movement. Howard himself was particularly influenced by Prince Peter Kropotkin's vision set out in 'Fields, Factories and Workshops' of self-governing communes. There had been earlier attempts to build model towns – Cadbury's Bourneville, Lever's Port Sunlight – and some of the great aristocratic estates had built pretty villages for their servants. But, however well-intentioned, these were all paternalistic dormitories for a workforce. Company towns. The brilliance of Howard's vision was that his Garden City would be a self-governing company run for the common wealth. What was astonishing was that he managed to get this idea, which wasn't going to be much of a benefit to anyone but the inhabitants, financed. Agricultural land was being sold at bankrupt prices and he managed to get a consortium to buy three moribund farming estates in a dull, clay-thick bit of Hertfordshire on the old Roman Icknield Way next to the medieval market town of Hitchin.

The Garden City movement held competitions to build a twentieth-century cottage for the new town. It had to be functional, aesthetic, sound, good quality and cheap. There were exhibitions which city people flocked to in droves to see what their future might look like. Light industry was supplied by Spirella, a now defunct firm that made corsets and bras.

In *To-morrow* Howard produced a diagram that is famous if you're interested in town planning. It was called the 'three magnets' and it showed the town, the country and this new place called town-country. Each 'magnet' had good and bad qualities. Town had social opportunity but also 'isolation in crowds', high wages, high rent, high prices, well-lit streets, slums, gin palaces, palatial edifices. The country had lack of society, but beauty of nature, woodland, meadow, forest, lack of amusement, bright sunshine, crowded dwellings and deserted villages. The third way had beauty of nature, social opportunity, fields and parks of easy access, low rents, high wages, low rates, plenty to do, low prices, no sweating, fields for enterprise, a flow of capital, pure air and water, good drainage, bright homes and gardens, no smoke, no slums, freedom and cooperation. I've edited the town and country's magnets, but the third way's list is as he wrote it. It's a marvellously idiosyncratic mixture of the practical, the parochial and the idealistic. Plenty to do, good drainage and freedom. And if you don't hear the authentic voice of England in that, you haven't been listening.

Letchworth was built in surprisingly speedy stages and was filled with third-way 'Tomorrow' people. One of its initial problems was the cost of housing. It all proved more expensive than they'd hoped, and too much for real workers – either industrial or rural – to afford. But their places were filled by Islington intellectuals and tweedy Utopians. Letchworth became a brave adventure for socialist radicals with a fondness for leather elbow patches, arts and crafts, medieval instruments, folk-singing, vegetarianism, hand-made clothes – often in the style of the fourteenth century – nonconformity, exhibitionism and single-issue obsessiveness. The self-consciously eccentric found a place where they were the norm.

The experiment in new living was practised in public with Morris dancing, open marriages, lesbianism, and pre-Christian religion. There was tireless willow-bending and corn-plaiting, rune-gossiping, well-dressing and solstice-bothering. New Age children with Celtic names did callisthenics in the street, common-law wives spun rough cloth on ancient looms and men stitched their own shoes and made jam and bras.

Letchworth became, briefly, a well-meaning if embarrassingly

barmy attempt at inventing a new way for a new century. It was
the first step on the long search for a New Age, and it was a very
moral one. The nineteenth-century received truth that alcohol
was the one defining evil of the working class was built into the
fabric of Letchworth. It was to be, uniquely in England, teetotal.
But there was a problem. It obviously had to have a pub – you
couldn't be an English town without an English pub. But the
new chaps of the third way, after a hard day's hoeing, weaving,
wood-cutting and corsetry, could go down to The Skittles for a
glass of ginger beer or a fortifying hot chocolate and a game of
skittles. Even when I was at school here fifty years later there was
still no pub, the only place that would serve you a drink was one
miserable hotel, and then you had to prove you were a bona fide
traveller.

It was easy to mock Letchworth and so many did, including
John Betjeman, who wrote a poem about it, 'Group Life'. The
home-made radicals soon moved on, all were subsumed into
probity, trimming their beards and practising supine naturism
whenever the steely wind out of Cambridgeshire permitted. The
Great War arrived when Letchworth was barely a teenager, and
that rather finished the hilarity of it all. By the Second World
War, it was all but indistinguishable from hundreds of other
satellite towns. Howard built one more in his own lifetime – the
ambitious Welwyn Garden City. Its clean, light factory was
Nabisco, the company that makes Weetabix. If you look on the
packet there's a little picture of Welwyn. Weetabix is a very
Garden City third way breakfast – bricks of wholesome brown
goodness. Form following function, that dissolves into a toothless mush.

Letchworth didn't disappear because it was a bad idea, or even
a flawed one, it was copied with alacrity by the rest of the
country – and then the rest of the world. There are Letchworths
everywhere. The cottages of Howard's original plan aren't
monuments or totems of modern design like the Bauhaus house,

because hardly anyone can live in a Bauhaus house, but Letchworth's cottages are everywhere. They're the shape of sunny, safe, sensible family homes, pebble-dashed, white-washed, pitch-roofed, half-timbered. They're the size and shape of the dreams and modest aspirations of most of us. Their decorative features are discreet, but the important thing is that their power is collective. These little, laughable, unremarkable homes came together to make a place that looks nice and polite, that values families and weekends and quiet pleasures; a place of trust and rectitude, freedom and co-operation with no sweating. You might also say of busybodies, silent snobbery, hidden perversion and quiet despair. They are, in short, the suburbs.

Most cities grow to be the image of huge boasts, the PR of wealth, built for the vanity and confirmation of power and sycophancy. Great cities are innately arrogant. They aspire to a municipal grandeur and stature that ignores or mocks the lives of most people who live in them. Great cities often look like the habitats of a recently vanished race of heroes and demigods, but provincial suburbs on the other hand are an accurate portrait of the people who live in them. They are an exact memory and memorial to the small achievements of real lives. That is their great beauty, their defining quality. It's also what makes them so obviously risible and embarrassingly irritating.

Howard had Blake's vision of a New Jerusalem and saw not another shining city of marble towers and granite halls, but a collection of improved workmen's cottages with a vegetable plot and a fruit tree. In the parks, instead of fountains to old gods and memorials to the dead, there would be maypoles and children's paddling pools, there would be ginger beer instead of champagne and honey for tea.

Howard's great insight, his humble genius, was to be one of the very few reformers who asked not: 'How can we improve the workers?' but 'What would the workers like?' Not: 'What does the mighty proletariat deserve?' but 'What could they live with?'

Howard is a member of a recognizable caste of English seer, self-effacing, humble, spectacled and tweedy; unremarkable, yet steely and stubborn in his resolve to do a good thing. It is England's luck that these men often appear at moments when other nations produce more bellicose and inflammatory doers. It's men like Howard who are the safety valves of England's anger, taking the temper and channelling its energy into something else: drains, gardens, cul-de-sacs and a beerless pub. Letchworth was and is a very English place for a very English plainness and contradiction.

St Christopher's, my old school, settled here in 1915 because the ethos and third way New Ageism was precisely what the strangely mystical and romantic founders wanted to instil into children. I remember one line from the school song: 'Christopher, Christopher, we are the pillars firm and white that stand beside the river.' I don't expect they sing it any more. It's a co-educational boarding school that was self-governing (with a single transferable vote, proportional representation before any country in the world had it). It was vegetarian and organic before ecology was a word, there were no uniforms and we called everyone from the headmaster to the smallest Montessori child by their first name even when I was there. It was a weird and unconventional place with a high proportion of Quakers, many of whom wore sandals all year round and one of whom wouldn't speak on Wednesdays in memory of those killed in Hiroshima.

Despite the crankiness, the long matted hair, the sallow cheeks, ragged jeans and wispy beards of the sixties, it was, underneath, just another English public school, albeit a rather benign one. It was freezing in the winter and cold in the summer. It smelt of vegetable farts, homo-erotica, games socks and the oil and sawdust mixture out of some Victorian work-house that we had to use to clean the floors. There was very little bullying, though I expect much unhappiness as at most boarding schools. We used that bizarre left-over language, born of dog-

Latin, that the private sector incubates – the Hindustani of the dorm, pidgin for lost boys: quis, ego, cavee and the obscure truncations and nicknames of places and things. We were taught nothing of the town or the school's place in it; we were each of us uninvited guests for six or seven years, but we behaved like a courted garrison. Letchworth was a place of utter disdain, a hideous troll nowhereville inhabited by ghastly common oiks. None of us lived in houses like that, or knew people who did; we didn't dress like them, eat like them or sound like them. The worst thing that could happen to us would be to end up like them – to leave school, but never make it to the station.

Our only official contact was semi-voluntary charity work on Sundays, handing out food parcels to the ancient and house-bound who were studiedly ungrateful, or just refused to answer the door to our sniggering patronage – that and the Saturday ritual of frisking the younger children for their weekly stash of New Age shop-lifting. The stuff that hadn't been eaten, broken or hidden would be returned with a curt apology.

All public schools, without exception, have this barely concealed distaste for their hosts. On the other side it's a solemn resentment that occasionally boils over into violence.

St Christopher's, with its hippy-alternative, Quaker-pacifist, non-competitive mission statement was not as bad as some, but I still remember the absolute sense of entitlement. We treated Letchworth with contempt, as if the whole place was hard of hearing and contagious. We were passionate about George Orwell and global socialism, and would play truant to go on marches against Vietnam and for abortion. I had pictures of Che Guevara and Trotsky on my wall, but Ebenezer Howard would have been an irony too far. I joined a new pressure group called Amnesty and collected half-crowns for political prisoners, Ian Smith's Rhodesia and Gulag Russia with a monstrous self-righteousness, but refused to see the hypocrisy of, at the very same time, calling the locals plebs and trolls and, that most damning abuse of the sixties, petit bourgeois.

As I walked back to school thirty years after having left I was once again struck by the aesthetic blandness of Letchworth. It's not even energetic enough to be ugly. Nerdy students of twentieth-century public housing might find some of the streets and crescents of passing interest, but the thing that makes it human-shaped and functionally admirable in theory also makes it hideously dull to be in. Fifty years of casual usage and cheap and cheerful shop-fitting has turned the high street into that predictable mix of charity shops, cheap discount chain stores and building societies. There are pubs here now, with charmless, sticky plastic rooms.

Spirella closed years ago, the fields that were Letchworth's green belt, where I smoked joints and felt around under bras, are now silent housing estates where the cul-de-sacs and closes are built with the same intention as Howard had a century ago, but without his vision or care. They're thin and mean and look temporary and cramped, and they don't have gardens you could grow your own cabbages in, they're the housing equivalent of polyester tracksuits. Again I can hear that old familiar sneer, tainting my observations. I notice with a raised eyebrow the Georgian-style carriage lamp, the classic garden ornaments, the pokerwork rustic house names, the boys turning lazy eights on their mountain bikes like big hamsters dressed in hoods and baseball caps, pretending this is south central Los Angeles, or Manchester, or Brixton, or even Luton, just anywhere less toytown than Letchworth.

However charitable and empathetic your viewpoint, Letchworth is still very ordinary. Nothing catches the eye or incites exploration. I remember that whilst at school the only place to eat with my parents – neither of whom drove – was the Wimpy, a fish and chip shop or an Italian restaurant above the cinema. We went there twice a term on exeat. It was always empty, but there were marvellous things on the menu – Tuscan hare, Parma ham, elaborate puddings. The manager was an excitable and effusive man, a very Italian Italian who welcomed my parents with histrionic pleasure, who wore tails and spongebag trousers and decorated the walls with framed paintings by his eleven-year-old son. I always felt embarrassed on his behalf, that this energetic, boundlessly hopeful, lonely man could come all this way and invest so much to sell homemade spaghetti to Letchworth. It was the first time I felt that neck-shortening, face-scrunching cringe at glimpsing England and the English through the eyes of a foreigner, but it wouldn't be the last. The restaurant's gone now and there's still nowhere to eat in Letchworth.

On my way back to the station I saw a squirrel. It was black. All my time at school I'd heard about these rare melanistic animals that were supposed to inhabit this little square of East England, but I'd never seen one, and here it was after all these years. Not really worth a special visit, but a good tick in your I-Spy book. It was nervily questing beside something else I'd forgotten, the roundabout – the very first roundabout in England. So right that it should be in Letchworth, spiritually kin to Howard's plan for a new rural urban people of the twentieth century. A brilliant little piece of social engineering that only works with the belief that others will behave well if you give them the option, that they'll see the point of the common good. The French and the Americans both tried roundabouts first, but rejected them. They could get their cars but not their heads around a roundabout. Their national temperaments didn't suit, but they were fine for the English. They are now the leitmotif of suburbia and the intricate embroidery of housing estates, pre-fabricated shopping centres, reinvented barns, bed and breakfasts, weekend kennels and stables, lay-by coffee huts, pick and pay polytunnel – all the ragged development that joins the dots of old villages and market towns throughout England.

This suburban sprawl of 'No Place' is also Howard's gift to us. In trying peacefully and non-judgementally to avoid the imminent smash and fracture and breakdown of his unfair society and to cure the sinful ills of the inner city and the bankruptcy of the country, he saw and planned a future that was so prescient that no one noticed he'd done it.

16

Nostalgia

Poundbury comes at you before you're ready for it. Like a coward in a bar fight, it smacks you in the eye as you're taking your coat off. Poundbury is Prince Charles's perfect English village, his brave effort to put his bricks where his mouth is. His answer to modernism and brutalism and minimalism and all the other hard-edged isms of post-war living. This is the way, he says, that most of us would like to live if we had a choice.

I'd always imagined it – and have often imagined it – as being a series of self-contained villas, humbly vaunting Utopia, set in that rolling, downy, somnambulistic England, that mind's-eye-shire that is the favourite backdrop of Victorian engravers. I imagined driving over a curly B road with double white lines and cresting a hill to see through a break in the carefully mixed deciduous wood, over a well kept but not too over-pruned hawthorn hedge, a glimpse of a distant Pickwickian huddle of thatch and nicotine stone, hugging a stately and elegant village church, wrapped in night-green yew trees. And I imagined that there would be horses and carriages, swains in smocks, and maids jerking double-fat gold top out of long-lashed Jerseys. I imagined men in red, back from fighting Boney in the Peninsula; I imagined drovers and day labourers and jolly curates and a grim sexton bowling and pall-malling outside the village pub. And perhaps a country wedding with rose petals, a bit of a local band with authentic instruments, the cooing of pigeons, the deafening hum of bees.

Then as we drew closer, driving down an ancient avenue of beech, chestnut and oak, we would begin to pass on the road a rag-taggle line of men and women walking toward the Poundbury of my imagination. There'd be a Viking and a monk arguing, a Saxon house-carl, a stern-looking Norman and a delicate maid with a long plait. Then there'd be Robin Hood and, on his charger, Richard the Lionheart. By the time we got to the sign saying: 'Poundbury, twinned with all our yesterdays' there would be men in top hats and side whiskers and a fat little queen, and Baden-Powell back from the African wars, and then, finally, local boys marching off to hang their washing on the Siegfried line. And that's the end, because that's the end of interesting history. After that it's all beastliness.

What we've driven past is the grand, moving tableau of England's rich tapestry, probably styled by Arthur Rackham. They've walked off the frontispiece of an Edwardian book called something like *Our Nation's Glory* for the nursery, or *Tales from our Island* for girls and boys who haven't started menstruating or masturbating yet. As each of the characters passes into Poundbury's miraculous purlieus, their costumes melt away and they morph into the men and women of today. They see us and they smile with conspiratorial winks as if to say, 'Don't let on, let this be our secret.' That's what I always imagined.

Poundbury isn't quite like that. You get to the edge of Dorchester and, bang, there it is. Not so much a village of timeless values and aesthetics, more an extension, a lean-to. There isn't so much as a thin strip of medieval fields between Dorchester and Poundbury; there is no moment to stop and take a view, straighten your tie and rub your shoe on your calf; you're right in the middle of it, and the first impression on a gusty, grizzled March Wednesday is that it is far, far nastier than you ever thought. The smart, urban, open-space minimal people with personality spectacles who close their eyes when they talk, who you imagined must have been over-egging metropolitan snobbery when they said it was quite, quite beyond anything, were understating the case. It is utterly beyond Dorchester in aspirational retro-tat.

The first mote to the eye is how crass, how boxily unsubtle the pastiche of Never Never village life has been. Most of you could have cut up old copies of *Country Life* and collaged a more winsomely attractive *mise en scène* than Poundbury. You walk around thinking that you must be missing something – is this all there is? What you're missing is what Poundbury's missing, a sense of purpose or identity. Really basic things are wrong – the scale, the relationship of the buildings to each other or to open space. Great lumps of vernacular have been blown up to make them contemporary functional, whilst others have been mini-aturized. What's most discordantly strange is that the buildings seem to be outgrowing themselves; windows aren't the right size for walls or doors; the scheme and rhythm of the whole place is aphasic. The pavement, for some unfathomable reason, is gravel – you crunch your way round scattering small stones onto the tarmac. It's not that the community has no heart, it has nothing else. We're walking round the cul-de-sacs and alleys that are ventricles of a heart that beats for nothing; there is no muscle, no limbs, no vital signs, no life. This isn't a model of how most people wish to live, it's something much smaller.

Above his tomb in St Paul's is Christopher Wren's epitaph: 'Reader, if you seek his monument, look around you'. This could be written in double yellow lines around Poundbury's round-about. What this is, is a self-portrait of Prince Charles: all his gauche good intentions with their strangulated awkwardness. Romance coupled with crass. Poundbury's both grandiose and small-minded. Stupendously arrogant and ever so humble.

You can see that taking the argument into the third dimen-sion and actually building a hypothesis in a field has a grand gestural sweep to it reminiscent of the other Prince of Wales, the Regent, building his shopping street and park and Brighton

Pavilion. But it's also a piece of blunt, stubborn vanity to expect real people to pay to be lab rats in an experiment which is really no more than a GCSE coursework debate on aesthetics. Compared with Regent's Park, Poundbury is a wendy house; compared with the vision of Albert's Great Exhibition or Edward I's Welsh castles, it's a garden ornament. But all that might have been excusable if it had actually worked, if Poundbury really were the way most of us want to live. But on the day I visited, there was a simmering row about the second stage of the village that was being constructed in a moribund field next door. The original experimental citizens resented the diluting of their exclusivity and, according to the people I asked up the road in Dorchester, they already looked down on the burghers of their larger and older neighbour.

Prince Charles has managed to grow a Petri dish of avaricious, purse-lipped, provincial snobs – how very, very House of Windsor. And in turn, he's turned his royal disappointment on them for thanklessly wanting to cash in on his good name and work by selling their ideal homes for a quick profit.

What's wrong with Poundbury is not the breeze block and stone cladding, the carefully regulated specimens in the garden, or the tasteful absence of satellite dishes, it's in its aspect; it faces the wrong way, it has its head turned over its shoulder and it looks lovingly at the past in a Canute-like attempt to stave off the beastly future. The olde England pastiches of Disney Florida are actually more successful and estate-agently honest than Poundbury because they don't have pretensions to be anything other than sentimental historiography. Poundbury is supposed to be both the way we lived and the way we should live. It refuses to contemplate any improvement or growth outside its own limited dead terms of reference. It's disappointed in and disapproving of the world it sits in, it implies a human spirit of quiet, repetitive craftsmanship as opposed to messy experiment, because nothing good, it says, can come of change. Unless it is the imperceptible inch-by-inch predestined certainty of an acorn turning into an oak tree.

Standing in the middle of this neurotic, irritably sighing, obsessively curated, wilfully blinkered suburb, you are irresistibly reminded of Prince Charles. He hasn't built a modern village for the overspill of Dorchester, he's constructed a monument to himself, to all the neuroses, night sweats and little articles of faith that bind Charles to his truncated role, the things that make Poundbury so nostalgically petulant. The overwhelming atmosphere of the place is his uncomfortable self-righteousness and self-pity. It cries out for a great clarion of arrogance, but what it comes up with is a little burp of conceit. Poundbury is an unconscious exercise in self-revelation. But unlike all the other royal builders, from William and his Tower of London to George and his Brighton Pavilion, Charles wouldn't dream of actually living in his creation. And that's ironically what makes it such a telling self-portrait. This is not a man at home in his own skin. He is our little Ozymandias. Poundbury is two trunkless feet dumped in Dorchester's back yard, 'Look on my works, ye Mighty, and despair!'

It is a neatly novel coincidence that Poundbury is a suburb of Dorchester, because Dorchester itself suffers from a severe case of looking back. This was once a sheep town, a hard, wild and woolly place on the southern English chalk down. It made a fortune from wool that was both big money and subsistence wages. There was life-sapping hard work and simmering rural resentment. Down here there were always recruits for a better tomorrow, for the overturning of society and the grand settling of moral debts. It was in this deceptively tranquil countryside that the first trade union, the Tolpuddle martyrs, met. Dorchester is where Hanging Judge Jeffreys held his Bloody Assizes.

Here were the desperate converts for new Edens, new orders, better tomorrows. Nonconformist religion was loud and judgemental down here. The Dorset and Hampshire chalk downs were crowded with tight rural communities that were blown back and forth from feast to famine by the agricultural economy. But today the landscape is eerily peaceful. The sheep have gone, the agricultural workers' delicately balanced lives expired. The countryside that supported Dorchester has been agri-cleansed, wiped clean into a dormitory retirement hush – a loss quite as devastating as the mine closures and heavy-industry amputations of the north. But down here in the south-west, there wasn't even the small solace of the flexi-time, self-employed assembly jobs that were used to bribe the old industrial landscape. There isn't even a motorway to Dorchester yet. Agriculture just stole away in the night. The great wealth and power of the land departed, and it was as if no one even noticed. Apart from Thomas Hardy, that is. In a series of novels, magazine articles and lyric-mulchy poetry, he did for Dorchester. He nailed the lid on its rough, rude coffin.

In a university somewhere someone is writing a thesis on the blight of writers in your landscape. No infestation of literature has been more devastating than Hardy's set work grasp on Dorchester. His Tess and Jude and all the Madding Crowd are a reoccupying force that will last a thousand years. Hardy wrote about the ending of traditional rural life in Dorset. He minded. His stories extolled its virtues, and its sad characters became tragic symbols of a continuous, organically-mystical romantic life that was already archaic and anachronistic when he set it to paper.

Hardy's love for Dorset stops the place from dying, but it also hooks it for ever in a moment. Dorchester is for ever Castlebridge. Here is the Far from the Madding café, the Return of the Native drop-in centre and assorted edible Wessexry, all invented and sugared by Hardy. There is nothing else for Hardy Country to do except sell his fudge and tea towels and bright little models of Julie Christie being shown the sabre cuts by Terence Stamp. Dorchester is pinned to a wall of nostalgia by Hardy's mawkish, depressing love of a vanishing life. But the irony is that the way of life caught in the aspic of his pen was anything but nostalgic. It was always looking for ways to improve itself, to get on and get out. The West Country was a crucible of new ideas and belief. Hardy's characters are constantly being caught by their pasts and tripped up by fate.

If I had to choose two words to inscribe on England's escutcheon, to tattoo onto its buttock, they would be 'schaden-freude' and 'nostalgia'. It never ceases to astonish me that there is no English word for those most English of emotions. An American pointed out that the English are the only people on earth who manage to feel *schadenfreude* about themselves. There is a long history of self-satisfied masochism in the English, a self-justifying pessimism. But it is nostalgia that is the most pernicious, enervating and tiresomely stereotypical English trait. Nostalgia is a word that only gained its current meaning in 1900, and only came into common usage by the thirties. What do you think they used before nostalgia? Do you think there's a lost word? Maybe we should go and find it and start using it again. Perhaps we ought to set up a little society with a committee and an honorary president for the protection of pre-nostalgia?

Nostalgia was originally a medical term, minted in 1756 for a mental sickness whose symptoms were acute longing for familiar surroundings. It was a debilitating home-sickness and apparently the people of Berne were especially afflicted by it.

What is it about the twentieth century that invented a need for a word for 'sentimental longing and regretful memory'? And why should it have touched such a nerve for the English? The turn of the nineteenth century was the peak of British power – politically, geographically, artistically, scientifically. The forty years from 1890 to 1930 were a great, blousy, blossoming of the English. They peaked. And it's remarkable how quickly it all dissipated and collapsed. The dissolution of empire was the background story of my childhood. Every other week it seemed there was footage of Princess Margaret or Lord Mountbatten in ostrich feathers pulling down the Union flag and raising something altogether gaudier to accompanying fireworks and native dancing.

The English took it all surprisingly well. The generation that had finally walked back to the pavilion and sold the family silver went about it with a resigned propriety, if not actually a good grace. So unlike the French, who broke all the pencils in the schools and fought hideous, petulant wars with a final explosion of spoilt temper and vindictive pettiness, walking off like husbands who'd just given ungrateful wives a bit of a slapping. The French turned their backs on the collapsed empire and felt only a twinge of resentment at the ingratitude. They got Camus and the European Community as a consolation. The French have a marvellous collective capacity for selective historical amnesia. After Suez, for instance, which for England and France was the great post-colonial pratfall, the globally awaited cathartic humiliation of two nineteenth-century powers, the French just shrugged, but the English trudged back with an almost unbearable loss of face, self-recrimination and sorrow.

The Empire broke England's heart, but it couldn't tell anyone. There was no one to confide in. It wasn't just the loss, it was the ugly shock that the Empire had wanted to dump them all along, couldn't wait to get out, to be rid of this groping old man. It was the realization that for all those years when they'd been waxing high romantic about service to the colonies, Anglo-Saxon blood draining into the sand in distant corners for the protection of savages and universal justice was a delusion. The Empire had been laughing at them behind their back. It gutted the English. Just as they were looking forward to a stately retirement, surrounded by the right sort of rosey remembrance, they found all was bitter and gall. And anyway, countries can't retire. There is no end to being a nation, though there is a beginning, as the freed empire was finding out.

The English experienced what everyone who has been dumped experiences – a cataclysmic, middle-aged stumble of self-confidence and nostalgia came to the rescue. Nostalgia was the panacea and the cold comfort. The deep past is a place that can't disappoint you, will never leave you. If you concentrate hard enough you can fold it round yourself, you can use it to muffle the present and confound the future, and that's what's so chronically depressing about all the Poundburys and all its fellow travellers, backward-looking restoration and preservation societies.

At the same time as the Empire was leaving, so the stately homes of England built on the wealth and avarice of industry, coal and colony were being demolished. In the forties and fifties dozens of country houses fell down or were pulled down as some poor sod of an elder son had to make the dreadful decision to walk away from a pile of stones that was the metaphor and simile of his duty and heritage and place in life.

The vile two-tier love of primogeniture is peculiar to England. Apart from being nastily eugenic it lands the genetically fav-oured boy with the sole responsibility for some hopeless, Jurassic pile of bricks and mortgaged parcel of rough grazing, which is deemed to be his lot in life. He's chained to the service of this leaky box because his father was and his grandfather got it for fiddling military procurement or gathering slaves or sending Welsh children down holes. Now he's indentured to being a janitor in his own home. Never able to do anything else, live anywhere else or have any money, just the hocked wealth of more damp rooms than he'll ever know what to do with. Forced to search out the sort of girl who'll put up with his unwinnable battle against decay and be sustained by the thin gruel of nostalgia.

Nostalgia is the new Empire, the virtual colonies. The foreign office of this zombie dominion is the National Trust. The Trust was set up at the apex of Empire by a trio of high Victorian reformers: Octavia Hill, Sir Robert Hunter and Canon Hardwick Drummond Rawnsley. They sound like Sherlock Holmes suspects. Octavia Hill was a formidable woman committed to the improvement of the lives of working people. She took over and ran slum housing projects and invented management techniques for public housing that went all over the world. She was a fierce advocate for maintaining small public parks for working-class people, so that, in her words, 'they could enjoy the healthy gift of air'. Such a marvellously Victorian patronizing idea that the air the lesser orders breathed was in someone else's gift – but that's unfair to her. Octavia was a committed social reformer who believed in the improving qualities – not just of fresh air, but of beauty, colour and culture. She was much influenced by Ruskin, as was Canon Hardwick Drummond Rawnsley – a muscular Christian with highly developed romantic stamina. He wrote 30,000 sonnets (a world record that is still uncontested) and worked for the preservation of wild landscapes, particularly the Lake District, along with Beatrix Potter. He was instrumental in acquiring the Trust's first property – Randel How Wood. Rawnsley and Hill are archetypal Victorians, steam-roller personalities driven by gimlet-eyed visions of the future. Hill, in particular, wanted the Trust to improve the living conditions of working people, Rawnsley was more interested in memorials to dead poets.

In the 120 years since the Trust was set up, it has grown into a parallel ghostly country within the country. It is the keeper of the heritage and soul of England. It has grown from a charity to provide fresh air for workers to being the biggest landowner in the nation after the Forestry Commission and Ministry of Defence, both of which are answerable to the people through Parliament. But the National Trust, with its 612,000 acres of English countryside and 600 miles of coast, defiantly claims to be separate from governments and state. It is answerable to no one but itself. It nods, patronizingly, to its 13 million visitors, 3 million paying members and 40,000 unpaid volunteers, but they have less power than penny shareholders in a public company.

The Trust has evolved into that very English organization, an apparently benign and supine charity whose main aim is the welfare of something unarguably worthy, like stray frogs, bruised children or pretty houses, but actually runs on unchecked to carve out a fiefdom within the nation that the Government would rather not get involved with.

Anyone who has ever seen the work of NGOs and charities in the Third World will recognize the National Trust. They don't throw their weight around so much as lean with it. The Trust's original purpose has been obscured by the size and complexity of the organization; the Oliver Twist rule of charity states that after a certain critical mass is achieved the purpose and motivation of the organization will be its own health and growth. So the National Trust has gone from being a means of providing respite and recreation for the working classes in salubrious surroundings, to the growth and maintenance of the National Trust itself. Its goodness and rightness are beyond argument; it is too large to be questioned. In fact, it is so large that the national good and the good of the Trust can be seen as synonymous. The National Trust stands as the keeper of the eternal soul of England, and what it says is good will be good. So it can ban dogs from beaches and dogs from foxes, it makes all sorts of country-defining decisions on the use of rural England, it decides how it should look and how it should behave and what we can do in it. Despite the Trust's supposed independence from Government, it accepts all sorts of grants for all sorts of work, including £263,000 from DEFRA to promote 'a greener lifestyle'. It is a great, weighty, well-connected and insistent pressure group on behalf of sustainable *bijou* chocolate boxes, lobbying for tax breaks for the owners and inheritors of pretty, expensive old things so that they can be kept in the houses that they happened to be found in, adding value to the buildings that the Trust will inherit in due course.

The Trust can evict families for the greater good of the public and will only accept some properties if they are entailed with enough money to sustain them. It regularly treads a morally unclear line when it comes to the wishes of owners and bequests which make up a thick slice of its annual £300 million income. That's an awful lot of tea towels and scones. But all this is as nothing, a few itches and irritations compared with the real, grim sickness of the National Trust. The Trust is hell. It's the pretty face and the sonorous voice of evil. What on earth did you think evil would look like? A flaming rubbish dump? A nuclear power station? A multi-storey car park? A pedestrianized town centre? A shanty town? No, the Trust and all its works is the real wickedness.

The nostalgia industry of heritage evil usurps the things of goodness and greatness and twists them into fear, inertia and doubt. Its mottoes are: 'For ever for everyone', 'The Trust's unique strength is the shared vision of our members', 'It offers the spirit of place', 'It's alive with history', 'There is a never-ending dialogue between the past, present and future', 'It offers visitors the real thing', 'The Trust is at the heart of managing the changes to the relevance of the past today and in the future'. What the National Trust actually says is that the best is all behind us, we will never be able to make or live as marvellously as our ancestors. All our endeavours from now on should be to preserve and lust over the stuff of the past. The National Trust is the church, not of the life you'll inherit, but the one you've missed. The one that's been squandered. Those hundreds and thousands of roped-off rooms with the motes of dust rolling through the dull light, past the faded silks and mottled gilding, or set about with unplayed harpsichords and unbummed sofas. The glasses that are never drunk from, the plates that are never eaten off, the unfucked beds, the childless nurseries, the kineless

byres, the horseless stables, the unlived homes, are all sets for a
ghostly reverie and the mawkish indulgence of bereft nostalgia.
The demoralizing daydream of wishing you were a dead person,
from a dead time, because it would be better than living now in
the salted present looking forward to a poisoned future. The
heritage industry and the mushy, soft, fearsome addiction to
nostalgia is more damaging and depressing to England and the
English than drunkenness or crime, or the collapse of ancient
values.

The Trust has moved out of stately homes and parks into
cottages, gardens and back-to-backs. This is supposed to be
egalitarian and meritorious, open and de-classed, a revision of
the past. In fact it's quite the reverse. It fixes the old class
structures in the aspic of heritage; it blesses it with the benign
gloss of nostalgia. When the tradition business was just grand
high art, it could be decoupled from the fat, worthy, thick
bastards who owned it. Indeed part of the argument for the Trust
was that it allowed the workers into the halls of the mighty, to
sup deep on the genius that was for everyone, but adding
miners' terraces and industrial workers' cottages adds a new
relativism. Their knick-knacks and worn utensils are not great art
or objects of beauty, they only have a resonance as part of the set
and the story, the plot of a perfect past. The patronage of
workers' lives moves the National Trust from being interested in
a national collection in terms of arts and crafts and admits that
what it's really preserving is a nostalgic other country.

Along with Poundbury, Prince Charles is setting up retrospective schools for drawing, design and architecture where students
can learn the old and unquestioned 'better' and unimprovable
way of doing things. The culture and artistic imperative of the
English has turned to being restorers and curators of their own
back catalogue. There can be nothing so completely empty, so
utterly soulless and bereft as to have to plagiarize your own
oeuvre.

I always thought that the most monstrously depressing culture I'd ever seen was Ancient Egypt. The sheer weight of effort devoted to death, the incalculable national waste of material energy and talent poured into morbidity. But it's beaten by the English Heritage industry. At least the Egyptians had the small consolation of death – a weird ritual afterlife to look forward to. The national mental illness of nostalgia and yearning for the comfort of imagined familiarity is far worse. It offers nothing but pretty regret. There is no hope in a National Trust England, no future. It's a perfect, ultimate nihilism. The individual is doomed always to founder on the marble example of his dead betters. The towering double-fronted irony of all this is that the times fixed in amber by the eternal chapel of nostalgia are the times when the English had the least respect for their yesterdays. They were the hell for leather gallop from Bosworth to the Blitz that was marked right up until the last furlong by an indiscriminate willingness to tear everything up and start again.

Every grand country house is built on the ruins of other houses, flattened for a grander vision. Every inch of England's landscape is some Englishman's belief that he can improve on God or some previous Englishman's vision. What would have happened to England if the National Trust had been set up in 1695 or 1395? The idea is laughable. It is inconceivable. The fuel, adrenalin and focus of greatness, of Empire, riches, intellectual excellence and artistic brilliance presumed that the best was always yet to come, that the future was an endless wonder. The past is rungs on a ladder. If you falter and look down, you're lost, which is exactly what the English have done. They're stuck with a paralysing vertigo, looking back from a great height at their past, too scared and traumatized by achievement to move up.

There was no word for nostalgia before 1900 because there was no need for one. Someone made a study of nostalgia once, asking people what they thought the optimum best time to have lived would have been. There are very few aspects of life that the

English don't think were better at some previous time; they all believe that the past was superior even in the face of statistics and histories that prove it wasn't. So there is the English truism that schools were better, hospitals healthier and, most commonly held of all, streets safer in some mystical, far-off past. What the study discovered was that the time most English consider happiest and safest was moveable. There was no consensus, but there was a formula. It was approximately twenty years before they were born, so the generation before yours lived in the halcyon time.

In fact what they were remembering was their own parents' childhood. We grow up listening to our parents talk about when they were kids. Adults romanticize and gild their youths; for their children it sounds like a magical age, a lost time. It instils a feeling that that was a golden age, and that our time is not as good or as much fun, and particularly not as straightforwardly simple or as safe.

There is a conceit that nostalgia and heritage are generally provincial, middle-class vanities. That metropolitan, creative, travelled and generously cultured people don't fall for the easy fix of the sentimental past. And you could point out that England undeniably has a very aggressive and confident modern artistic life: in music, literature, poetry, design and architecture there is much being produced and conceived that is classy and solid and original and modern. And it goes right across the waveband from high to popular. But if you look and listen and read carefully you'll notice how much of it is revivalist and retrospective, how much the new takes on an older theme, how much of England's aesthetic of the last hundred years has been plundering the national coffers. The culture reprises itself.

I seem to have been through at least three sixties revivals since my first job working in Carnaby Street actually *in* the sixties. In each one the force grows weaker and the irony bulkier, the toothless old lion's-share of English culture is taken up with genuflecting to, or kicking the shins of, English culture. It's just as much about heritage and nostalgia as dressing up in the Sealed Knot, or paying five quid to imagine you're a Georgian countess in some gloomy stately home. National nostalgia is not all reverie and sadness for things lost and an incomprehension for the present, it isn't just stalled confidence and the loss of a role; it's what happens when history mounts you from behind.

History is England's thing, England's pride. England has embroidered a longer and more elaborate story than almost any other country, but there comes a point when as a group, as a nation, you disappear under the weight and gaudiness of your own heritage. Like those Celtic kings who would recite the names of their ancestors whenever they met someone new, the English have lost the sense of who they are without the national family tree. And for a generation now they have gone from making history to curating it. There is a fulcrum, a tipping point, where the very thing that was the energy that propelled the country forward now becomes the dead weight that holds it back. Something similar happens to culture. The confidence the English derived from the empire of creativity that was always larger, grander and more impressive than their geographical, political and economic dominions, and over which the spotlight never set, has grown to be a huge rucksack of responsibility. Every performance or creation of a new work is an audition in front of an invisible committee, stretching back to Chaucer. The dual responsibility of both tending the demanding canon of the past whilst trying to create something plausibly, lustfully contemporary grows too much and art becomes pastiche and revival. Original work is all too apologetically slight and arch, as if it didn't want to disturb the tombs or risk being drowned out by the turbine howl of spinning in graves.

The grist of nostalgia leads to yet another variation of English irritation: the fruitless, negative, retrospective, pissed-offness with things that ain't what they used to be. The trains, roads, policemen, postmen, doormen, men's tennis, television, comedies, war films, newsreaders, weathermen, weather, manners, respect, pubic hair, hats, buttons, underpants, spectacles, linen, fresh air, boats, toy soldiers, kites, fountain pens, notepaper, round pin plugs, blankets, lawns, lawn mowers, roses, summers, Christmas; the taste of tea, of milk, of bread, marmalade, eggs, sausages, greengages, raspberries, penny chews, hard toffee, seaside rock, Victoria sponge, stout, accents, breasts, bottoms, tongues, heels, kidneys, bacon, ham, mutton, chicken, salmon, tinned peaches, tripe, pork pie, milk, cream, cheddar, kaolin and morphine; the smells, the lost smells of cars, ladies, lily of the valley, mackintoshes, gumption, coal, fog, pencil sharpeners, Vick, cherry blossom, Swan Vestas, cafés, first-class carriages, anti-macassars; and the noises vanish to the echo, the sound of police sirens, church bells, factory hooters, civil servants, dailies who did, newspaper sellers, football rattles, two-minute silences, larks, cobbles, harmonicas, whistling, mono, the World Service, cellophane, Sunday mornings, and the touch, the lost touch, the feeling of tweed, darned socks, woollen vests, door knobs, light switches, ribbed medicine bottles, pairs of hair brushes, lino, carving sets, bus seats, skin that had never seen the sun. You can play this game indefinitely. It makes for an exciting, old-fashioned family pursuit on long car journeys – preferably in a shooting brake. Just make a list of decline and you'll be astonished by how many things a five-year-old can name that were better in his youth.

The English get their yearning for nostalgia at the breast, except that it's probably the bottle these days – put that on the list. You have to be English to play, of course. The other joy of the nostalgia game is that it's a shibboleth to all other nations. They have absolutely no idea what you are on about or, more germanely, why.

The most depressing and dispiriting facet of the national

nostalgia neurosis is the diaspora of the environmental movement. The English, in particular, find a grim pleasure in rarity
and extinction. The passing of habitat. They suck their teeth
with a delicious sadness and revel in the hand-wringing.
Mourning becomes the English. The vanishing environment,
the destruction and change – all for the worse of course – give
the generation who have a natural political antipathy to the
conservatism of yearning for Empire and global muscle an
opportunity to join in the English game of nostalgia.

Environmentalism is the grandest, most all-encompassing
form of heritage reconstruction because at its heart and in its
soul it knows that there is a right way for the world to be and
that we've passed it. There was, some time behind us, a pristine
moment of balance, renewal and sustainability that we need to
get back to, or at least try to recreate in parts so that everything
from houses to vegetables, transport, underpants and facial hair
needs to be at least pre-twentieth century and preferably pre-
seventeenth century. With all this goes a reverence for communities of people who are primitive. They are not seen to be lagging
behind the rest of us, despite what they themselves might think,
they are, for the environmental nostalgic, in fact walking us back
to happiness and harmony. It is a given that the further back you
are from the twentieth century, the closer you are to Eden, and
therefore the ignorant and the inexperienced have much to
teach us.

This isn't an argument about the specifics of environmental
change. It's not about the denial of global warming or the waste
of water or the use of chemicals or erosion, pollution, inequit-
able trade and cruel farming and all the rest of the smorgasbord
of earthly concern, it's simply a disappointment and a disgust
with the natural position that the English as a community take
when confronted by the fight or flight of the environment –
they've decided to run for the past. The emotional safety and
comfort of their safe, romanticized dead place.

Many things about the English are eternal, ingrained in their hard growth rings, characteristics that make them. But this fear of the future is new and it's quite the opposite of what the people who brought them up believed. The English used to know that the answer to everything was ahead of them, that it could be achieved by bravery, ingenuity, intelligence and the collective will. If you slice history like a ham there will be places where you're dead wrong, but for the long stretch it's about the rightness of being who you are. The modern nostalgics have made progress a damned and dirty word, but it was always at the very heart of the English belief in themselves, and whether you think it good or ill, progress continues, despite your best intentions. Tomorrow is always going to be what happens next. You can be for it or you can be agin it, but either way, that's where you're going.

The most contemporary expression of English nostalgia is the Green Movement. It may seem to be a country mile from the prosaic nostalgia of stately homes, but it's just as fear-bound and querulous. The Green Movement is predicated on the belief that everything's going wrong and it's our fault. What we must do is put it right, and to do that we have a choice. We either go back to a point before it went wrong, or we go forward and progress our way through whatever the future holds.

If you set aside the assumptions and predictions, the second-guessing of all the interested parties, and just take this choice as being a philosophical one, a test of collective will, it simply comes down to going back or going on. The Green Movement, whatever its rights and wrongs, has proved to be the test of character for the English, and it's funked the challenge. Its answer has been to turn back. There is a nostalgic belief in some perfect time of mutual co-existence amongst all things, a decade, a century, a week, a moment of seamless interlocking circles of consumption, of production, well-being and limited expectation, of utility and spirituality, that we should try to reprise.

The other choice is to trust the thing that got us this far, our brains, our ingenuity and inquisitiveness and the blessed luck of our species. The definition of those who want to save the world and those who are blindly setting out to destroy it is defined by going back to safety or forward to Armageddon. As a rule, I distrust people who lard their arguments with the assumed opinions of the dead, but I do think that confronted with the same problems and the same choices, every English generation from Bosworth to the Blitz would have voted unequivocally to go forward, trusting in their Englishness, their ability to adapt, to be ruthless, tough and cunning. To be greedy and clever. The English believed not just in themselves, but that providence had a special place for them. To go back and try and unpick progress, to re-label achievement as exploitation and destruction is a spectacular act of national desecration; quite apart from the merits or realities of environmental concern, this sudden cataclysmic failure in confidence is quite unique for the English.

Thomas More wrote *Utopia* as a satire of his time, which was perhaps the most spectacularly bullish, destructive and precipitously confident of all English moments. Up close More saw chaos and the wilful destruction of a world he thought divinely ordered. All the pieces were being thrown in the air and no one could know where they would fall. Utopia passed into the language and into the English psyche as some sort of destination. It pops up again and again in Blake, in the loonies and mystics and hard-working muscular Christians who built schools and poorhouses and drains and bridges, who set up ideal towns in un-ideal corners of the colonies. The private secret snap of a Utopia is something the English would carry in their wallets – until now, that is. Until the Greens and the environmentalists told them that all the Utopias were in the past.

The English on a roll with a fair wind, a big idea and a gust of ego may be infuriating, but they're nothing like as pathetically annoying as when they're doubting, contrite, whinging and frightened.

The correct nostalgic wisdom is that, as a species, we have forgotten more than we've learned, and that what we've misplaced was deep and eternally useful and what we've picked up and kept is flashy, gimcrack and shallow. Lord Clark of Civilization, a man who spent his entire life protecting and curating heritage – though he would have wrinkled his epicurean nose at anything as tacky and saccharine as nostalgia – once said that his favourite quotation was German. It translated as: 'If we do as our fathers did, we don't do as our fathers did.' On first meeting it sounds Krautishly opaque, but persevere and it becomes, in a Teutonic head-furrowed way, quite profound. And it couldn't be more appropriate for the English; to repeat something is not to recreate it, every action is new within the context of its time.

Afterword

The mountain people of Kentucky have remained true to their breeding and root stock like wild roses. Their mountain fastness has maintained and protected a recognizable, prickly English-ness. They have bred too close but true to type. There is none of the cultural preciousness of expatriate communities, fearful of assimilation and loss of identity, who guard their breakfast, hats and nursery rhymes as if they were the eternal flames of identity.

Culture is not who you are, it is a symptom of who you are. People aren't what they make, they are how they make what they make. By forgetting their origins and not giving a damn about assimilation or identity, the mountain people have remained more authentically themselves than any green-bowlered, begorra-ish, Danny Boy-sobbing Boston-Irish.

The Kentucky English imply a truth about the country over the water. They are a distant mirror, perhaps the portrait in the attic. In 200 years, the mountain community has lived a life of god-fearing aggressive hardship. It has sung brittle and beautiful songs, worked hard at simple tasks, maintained close inverted communities and discouraged the enquiry or interference of outsiders. It has survived in rudimentary and admirable ways, but its people cannot, by any measure, be said to have prospered or been terribly successful. In the land of great opportunity, during the centuries of greatest expansion, they grasped hand-to-mouth farming and depression industry exploitation and held it tight. As a community, they did markedly worse than other communities, except those that had been slaves or illegal immigrants.

It's not that the English per se didn't do well in America. Individually they were the most successful group in the New World, providing more of the great and the good than any other immigrant group. Famously, English beat German to be the official language of America by the narrowest of votes. English ideas and laws, institutions and aesthetics account for a great deal of what America became, so why is it that the Hillbillies remain so stuck, so little evolved? It would seem that the English, when left alone to mature and fester in their own prejudices and sweaty sharp characteristics, aren't the energetic opportunity exploiters, mercurial inventors, canny manipulators and silver-tongued convincers the old island story would have us believe. Left to their own devices, they revert to being stuck, prickly peasants and good soldiers. What eastern Kentucky seems to prove is that the English need to be diluted, mixed in, to work properly. In the rest of America they have been one part in so many. When the English had America to themselves it all looked a bit like Kentucky; it was the masses of others that actually supplied the intellectual, social, economic and relaxed freedom to the Land of the Free.

Back in England the ability and the habit of getting on and forging the future, the massive, blustering confidence that drove the English, seems to be due to regular injections of others' new ways of being and seeing and doing. The mythical forging of the English, the coming together of Norman, Saxon, Celt and Scandinavian, is said to have created the magical alloy. The truth is that the mixture was never finished. It continues to degrade and rust back unless it has constant additions of otherness: Lombards and Flemings, Jews, Huguenots, Germans, Dutch, Bengalis, Punjabis, West Indians, East Africans and New Europeans. Plus, of course, the continual drizzle of Irish and Scots.

The English, left on their own, are some of the most objection-able people you could wish to avoid. They have a unique national habit of bringing out the worst in each other. I can't think of any other nation that has to be separated from itself for its own good – every collection of five Englishmen needs a foreigner to stop it becoming a social health hazard. England and Englishness are not a matter of geography or weather, or fortuitous position in the Atlantic, they are genetic Marmite – a little bit of them goes an awful long way.

Their story, the honours and the achievements and the gifts, is remarkable, as is the fact that so much bounty and opportunity should have improved them so little, made them so impervious to fondness, so uncomfortable in their own skins. The pugna-cious people caught between the cliff and the wall have a peculiar, stringent, collection of attributes. They have also been the recipients of a great deal of good luck, just when luck was needed.

Nations and people are all transient, they flicker, flare and fade. The English will queue politely with mounting irritation to go hand in hand to oblivion, to join the Celts and the Picts, the Beaker people and the thousands of wandering weavers, mud-coilers and bone-carvers whose collective names are known only to their forgotten gods. The conundrum of the English character will be tipped into the pool of our species as the leavening in someone else's make-up, a strand of some new people. And when, in a distant millennium, a child stands with his arms crossed and a face like thunder, stubbornly refusing to budge, his mother will look at him with incomprehension and say, 'I'm sure I don't know where he gets it from.'

INDEX

UR OPERA
PLAY ST
RN WITHIN
AR PARK FULL G
RIES NOT INCLUDE
ON LOST IN TR
T INCL
L CL
DOGS
THE GA
RIKES PLEASE QU
HILDREN ALL
SED ALL OUR OPERA
VE SPEE
NO STOPPI
EED CA   RESPASS
LUN   POSI   CLOSED NO
E S RIKES DIVERSION AHEAD
THE GRASS NO ENTRY CCTV
STRICTIONS IN OPERATION LEAVES ON
WAITING WITHIN ONE HOU